Relevant Reading
Evaluating Today's Issues

by Delana Heidrich

illustrated by Milton Hall

cover illustration: Don Ellens

Publisher
Instructional Fair · TS Denison
Grand Rapids, Michigan 49544

ISBN: 1-56822-424-9
Relevant Reading
Copyright © 1997 by Instructional Fair • TS Denison
2400 Turner Avenue NW
Grand Rapids, Michigan 49544

Table of Contents

About This Book

The activities in this book were designed to motivate students to think and write critically about their own reactions to readings such as those they will encounter in the real world. Editorials, advice columns, newspaper articles, speeches, advertisements, letters, government reports, commentaries, and more are all included. Each lesson addresses a topic of concern to today's youth presented in a straight-forward, easy-to-use format that includes Background, Student Reading, Understanding the Reading, Teaching Activities, and Extensions.

The Background of each lesson provides the teacher with a historical perspective of the lesson's topic, an overview of the present-day status of the topic, and a look at its possible future. It is suggested that the teacher use the background information to become acquainted with the topic and to share parts of it with students.

The Student Reading is the editorial, letter, speech, advertisement, or other reading that students are assigned. The Student Reading serves as a starting point for discussions, extensions, and other activities.

Understanding the Reading contains questions students should be able to answer following the reading of the student page. The purpose of Understanding the Reading is to check student comprehension of the reading only—not to address the more important issues found in the teaching activities and extensions.

The Teaching Activities are reproducible activities that stimulate critical thinking and creativity; they encourage students to express their own thoughts about the specific lesson.

The Extensions section suggests activities and research that make the topic of the lesson more tangible to students. The Extension ideas take students beyond the pencil and paper and into the library, science lab, or some other hands-on realm of creativity.

Discussing and sharing of thoughts and ideas among students is the key issue to the success of the activities in this book. The topics alone should stimulate lively discussion and encourage students to analyze their own thinking and values on some of the most widely discussed issues.

Background

Students examine what it means to be prepared for today's world of business when they read a letter from a top executive to his former high school principal.

Education in the Information Age

In this, the Information Age, when graduates of the year 2000 can expect to learn more in their senior year of high school than their grandparents learned in their entire lifetimes, education is taking on a whole new face. Although children continue to be instructed in basic math and science skills and to gain traditional knowledge of history, literature, and the arts, their teachers are quickly transforming from know-it-all sages into mentors who assist students in the mastering of research and problem-solving skills—especially as they pertain to our world's ever-changing technology. As the planet's body of knowledge grows larger by the minute, it is no longer possible to learn all there is to know, even in a single field of study. Today's students need not concentrate on knowing everything, but rather on knowing how to access the knowledge they do need when they need it and how to adapt to an ever-changing, ever-growing body of knowledge. Today's graduates need to be life-long learners.

Understanding the Reading

Following a reading of the businessman's letter to his former principal, students should be able to answer the following questions:

1. What are the four pieces of advice Mr. Pursley offers schools in educating today's youth? (basic computer skills, basic skills exams, varied classes, life-long learners)

2. What assessment system does Mr. Pursley suggest should replace the 4.0 grading system? (a competency system in which students show mastery of knowledge on basic skills exams)

3. Why do you suppose Mr. Pursley would take the time to write this letter to his former principal? (He has strong opinions about what skills graduates will need to be successful in the business world.)

Teaching Activities

1. We have entered the Information Age. Does that change the goal of education today? Are there some subjects that used to be essential that are no longer necessary because of the presence of technology? Are there some skills that were once not important for the average person that are essential today? Allow students to think critically on the role of education in the Information Age by completing the "What All Do I Have to Know, Anyhow?" activity with a partner.

2. American education has changed over the past few decades. Jobs that were commonly held in the 1950s no longer exist today. Skills and knowledge necessary today were not even taught to many of the parents of today's youth. Require students to work with an adult to complete a chart on the differences in jobs and education between today's world and the world of the 1950s with the "Education Then and Now" activity.

Extensions

1. Assign students to write a letter to their own principal outlining their opinions of what should be taught in schools today.

2. Have students work in groups to research various eras in American education. Discuss when and why public education started in the United States and what educational trends have come and gone and why. As an alternative, some students may wish to research education in other parts of the world (present or past).

3. Read about frontier schools of the 1800s in *Immigrant Kids* by Russell Freedman (Scholastic Inc., New York, 1980) or about children at work before the child labor laws in *Kids at Work: Lewis Hine and the Crusade Against Child Labor,* also by Russell Freedman (Scholastic Inc., New York, 1994).

4. Today there is a raging debate among educators, parents, and politicians about how best to educate the youth of today in preparation for the world of tomorrow. Some schools are trying the separation of the sexes at the middle school level. Some schools are trying the one-room schoolhouse approach again, allowing older and younger students to work together. Private schools and many public "magnet" schools specialize in one field. Other schools are trying a back-to-the-basics approach. Many schools are making extensive use of technology in the classroom and look to the day when children will learn via the computer. Many schools have tried altering their calendars or schedules to meet the demands of today's world. One senator in Colorado even suggests that allowing children to decide whether or not they want to go to school will improve schools for those who do attend. Assign the writing of an essay on what students think the best educational situation would be for today's youth. They may combine ideas listed above or think of their own.

318 Park Place
Turtletown, Iowa

Mrs. Hissong, Principal
Fairfield High School
Omaha, Nebraska

Dear Mrs. Hissong:

As a past graduate of your school and a successful businessman in a position to hire present graduates of your school, I offer you—and all American schools—the following advice:

First of all, teach your students the basics in computer technology. I have no use for computer illiterate employees. Second, demand that your students have a mastery of the basics. Get rid of the 4.0 grading system and simply require that *all* students pass basic competency exams in reading, writing, and mathematics. I do not ask applicants for their grade point average; I ask them to pass reading, writing, and math tests before I consider them for employment. Next, offer your students a variety of classes from art appreciation to auto mechanics. A well-rounded person—one who looks at the world from many different angles, is willing to take risks, learn new skills, try many different solutions to a problem, and compromise with colleagues and customers when necessary—is a person whom I would hire. Most importantly, teach your students problem-solving and research skills. In this, the Information Age, my field—and every other field—changes from minute to minute. I need employees who are not afraid to work with new information and to come up with new answers to new problems. When you send students out of your doors and onto my doorstep, and other doorsteps in the business world, send people who have a mastery of basic skills and who are willing to be life-long learners, and I will place them in good jobs.

Sincerely,

Mr. Timothy A. Pursley

What All Do I Have to Know, Anyhow?

Discuss and answer the following questions with a partner. Be prepared to share your answers with the class.

1. Which school subjects do you expect will be of value in your adult life? Why?

   _____

   _____

2. Which school subjects do you expect will be useless in your adult life? Why?

   _____

   _____

3. What does it mean to be living in the Information Age? Do great advances in technology and science mean you need to know different things from what your parents needed to know when they left high school?

   _____

   _____

   _____

4. What does it mean to be an educated person in today's world? What do you think it meant to be an educated person twenty years ago? Fifty years ago?

   _____

   _____

   _____

5. What does it mean to be a life-long learner? Do today's graduates need to be prepared to be life-long learners? Why or why not?

   _____

   _____

   _____

6. Is the 4.0 grading system a good way to evaluate student learning? What other ways might student knowledge and mastery of basic skills and problem-solving techniques be assessed?

   _____

   _____

   _____

Education Then and Now

Ask an adult about American education in the 1950s and then complete the following chart which compares the occupations and education of the 1950s to those of today.

Five Common Jobs
in the 1950s

1.

2.

3.

4.

5.

Five Common Jobs
Today

1.

2.

3.

4.

5.

Necessary Skills and Knowledge
in the 1950s

1.

2.

3.

4.

5.

Necessary Skills and Knowledge
Today

1.

2.

3.

4.

5.

Classes Taught in School
in the 1950s

1.

2.

3.

4.

5.

Classes Taught in School
Today

1.

2.

3.

4.

5.

Nutrition Through the Ages

Background

Nutrition is the process of taking in and using food. It is important to the body's maintenance and growth.

Early in the history of humanity, hunters and gatherers ate what they could when they could. They were not concerned about digesting too many (or the wrong kind of) preservatives because all of their foods were eaten immediately. They were not concerned about the intake of excess fat, because the fat they consumed was necessary to keep them going until their next meal.

Today advanced methods of growing, preparing, and preserving foods have made a wide range of food choices available to many of us. In today's world with so many choices, time constraints, and other reasons, busy lifestyles are responsible for many people making poor food choices. Yet when a person does not get vitamins, minerals, proteins, fats, and calories in the proper balance, he or she can be faced with severe diseases, obesity, or even starvation. More often, however, the effects are not so extreme. Many people eat a varied enough diet to meet their basic needs but still feel tired or generally in ill health, conditions that can be traced to their food choices.

In this lesson, students read, discuss, and write about personal diet choices.

Understanding the Reading

Following a reading and evaluation of Gina's menu for the week of February 4-10, students should be able to answer the following questions:

1. Did Gina's diet include a variety of foods from each of the food groups? (No, it especially lacked fresh fruits and vegetables.)

2. Did Gina eat any green, leafy vegetables during the week reported? (No)

3. Was Gina's caloric intake appropriate for a young woman? (Answers will vary as do estimates of appropriate caloric intakes, but Gina was probably ingesting a fairly appropriate number of calories each day.)

4. Gina's diet did not lack calories. What *was* Gina's diet lacking? (the vitamins and minerals found in fresh fruits and vegetables)

5. Do you think Gina's diet could be responsible for her fatigue? Why or why not? (Answers will vary.)

6. If Gina supplemented her diet with a multi-vitamin, would she be likely to feel better? (Perhaps, but remind students that vitamins—and especially some minerals that are found in minute, but necessary, amounts in fruits and vegetables are not found in multi-vitamins.)

Teaching Activities

1. Assign the completion of "My Food Choices This Week." Discuss the results in class. Was this a "typical" food week for students? Why or why not? Did most students eat foods from each of the food groups each day? About how many calories did each student consume each day? What did students learn from taking a conscious, in-depth look at their food choices for a week?

2. Should doctors consider nutritional factors more often in diagnosing illnesses? Will humans ever take a nutrient pill instead of eating? Why or why not? Allow students to think critically about their food choices and the food choices of others by assigning the completion of the "Nutrition and Health" activity.

3. People often eat more than one serving of a food without knowing it. Allow students to look up the amount of food in a single serving with the "How Much Is Enough" activity.

Extensions

1. Divide students into groups of three or four. Assign the research, reporting, and presenting of information on various modern-day eating disorders.

2. Have students collect favorite recipes from friends and relatives or create some of their own to be included in a class recipe book.

3. Research the different types of foods eaten around the world. Why are various foods popular in various locations? Try some foreign recipes in the classroom.

4. Grow a garden on school grounds.

Dear Gina,

Because all of your tests came out negative, I believe it may be possible that your fatigue and general ill health might be traced to your diet. Please record below *everything* you eat for one week and bring this form with you to your next appointment.

Sincerely,

Dr. Bonnie Miller

Dr. Bonnie Miller

Gina Brown, Age 20. Nutritional Record
Actual Menu February 4-10

Monday

Food	Amount
sugar donuts	2
coffee	1 cup
burrito	1
diet cola	1 can
spaghetti/sauce	2½ cups
garlic bread	1 cup
coffee	1 cup
ice cream	1 cup

Tuesday

Food	Amount
corn flakes	1½ cups
milk	3/4 cup
coffee	1 cup
ham sandwich	1
potato chips	½ cup
diet cola	1 can
pork chops	2
applesauce	½ cup
mashed potatoes	½ cup
gravy	¼ cup
corn	½ cup

Wednesday

Food	Amount
coffee	1 cup
raisins	½ cup
diet cola	1 can
fish	1 steak
rice	½ cup
peas	½ cup

Thursday

Food	Amount
granola bars	2
coffee	1 cup
cheeseburger	1
French fries	½ cup
diet cola	1 can
ham	1 steak
mashed potatoes	½ cup
applesauce	½ cup
ice cream	3/4 cup

Friday

Food	Amount
Corn flakes	1½ cup
milk	3/4 cup
granola bars	2
diet cola	1 can
lasagna	1 cup
garlic bread	1 slice
banana cream pie	1 slice
lemonade	1 cup

Saturday

Food	Amount
bacon	4 slices
eggs	2
toast	2 slices
coffee	1 cup
sugar donuts	2
turkey sandwich	1
potato chips	3/4 cup
diet cola	1 can
fried chicken	2 pieces
French fries	½ cup
corn on the cob	1
banana cream pie	1 slice

Sunday

Food	Amount
coffee	1 cup
sausage	3 links
toast	2 slices
omelet	1
roast beef	3 slices
mashed potatoes	3/4 cup
carrots	3
chocolate cake	1 slice

My Food Choices This Week

List below all of the foods you eat for one week. After completing the "How Much Is Enough?" activity, come back to this page and see whether the servings you eat are considered single servings. Do you eat a varied diet?

Monday

Food	Amount

Tuesday

Food	Amount

Wednesday

Food	Amount

Thursday

Food	Amount

Friday

Food	Amount

Saturday

Food	Amount

Sunday

Food	Amount

Nutrition and Health

The following questions have been designed to help you focus on your own food choices and the food choices of others. Reflect on the questions presented and then answer them on a separate sheet of paper. Be prepared to share your answers with others in your class.

1. Should doctors consider nutritional factors more often in diagnosing illnesses and prescribing the means for a cure?

2. Can a person meet all vitamin and mineral needs from supplements, or is it necessary to get them from food sources?

3. Will we ever get to a point where humans will take nutrient pills that hold all that is necessary for life instead of eating food? Why or why not?

4. What factors play a role in your food choices? Do you read labels and consider the nutritional and caloric value of your meals and snacks?

5. Do you make different food choices when alone, with friends, with family, on weekends, at parties, and in the summer months?

6. Do you think males and females consider different factors in making their food choices? Do males and females have different nutritional needs?

7. Have you ever been on a specific diet? If so, did you check with your doctor first? Did you diet at the request of a parent, friend, doctor, or of your own choice?

How Much Is Enough?

Eating a varied diet is only half the battle to a healthy diet. The other half is eating the foods in the proper amounts. On the packages of all prepared foods, you will find what is considered the amount of that food an average person should eat to make up one serving. All the other nutritional information listed on the package refers to that amount of food. Many people eat far more than one serving of such things as cereal or potato chips without even being aware they are doing so. Look at food labels and/or calorie counter books or charts and list the amount of food that makes up a single serving for the food categories listed below.

AMOUNT THAT MAKES
UP ONE SERVING

Five Types of Cereal

_____   _____

_____   _____

_____   _____

_____   _____

_____   _____

Five Vegetables

_____   _____

_____   _____

_____   _____

_____   _____

_____   _____

Five Snack Foods

_____   _____

_____   _____

_____   _____

_____   _____

_____   _____

Five Dessert Foods

_____   _____

_____   _____

_____   _____

_____   _____

_____   _____

Background

Although various societies have punished criminals in numerous ways throughout history, the United States today relies heavily on incarceration in dealing with those who break the law. In fact, a higher percentage of Americans is incarcerated today than in any other civilized country. America imprisons violent and nonviolent offenders: murderers, rapists, embezzlers, and con men.

Punishment: Past, Present, and Future

Penologists and reformers disagree on what the motives of punishment are. Some contend that punishing a criminal deters others from attempting similar crimes. Others suggest that criminals must be locked away in order to protect law-abiding citizens.

Originally, prisons were intended to provide for rehabilitation in addition to addressing these and other motives of punishment. Yet the penologists and reformers agree that with the presence of gangs and the overcrowded conditions, prisons are no longer places of rehabilitation. So, is a prison sentence still the best alternative for punishing one who chooses to break the law?

In this lesson, students make personal judgments about the effectiveness of incarceration today and suggest possible alternatives for the future following the reading of a newspaper columnist's history and opinion of imprisoning criminals.

Understanding the Reading

Following a reading of Mr. Ericson's essay, students should be able to answer the following questions:

1. What three forms of punishment did primitive societies use? (social disapproval, restitution to victims, exile from tribe)

2. Initially, what did prisons hope to do in addition to punishing criminals? (They hoped to reform criminals with the teaching of morals and discipline.)

3. Why do criminals seldom become rehabilitated in American prisons today? (overcrowded conditions and the presence of gangs and violence inside prisons)

4. Does the author of this article believe that the answer to all crimes is imprisonment? How do you know? (No, the final paragraph of the article pleads for citizens to consider alternatives to imprisonment and to think about the reasons behind deviant behavior today.)

Teaching Activities

1. Teachers often try to create a behavior management system in the classroom where the consequences for misbehavior fit the misbehavior. Allow students to think about what appropriate punishments for various real-world crimes would be if the punishments were to fit the crimes. "The Consequences of Crime" activity sheet gives students space to record their thoughts.

2. Ask students to work in groups to think critically about some issues that are not directly brought up in the newspaper article, but that pertain to punishment and imprisonment by assigning the completion of "Punishment, Restitution, Rehabilitation, or Revenge?"

Extensions

1. As an entire class, write a letter to the editor of a local newspaper addressing the issue of the growing prison population in America. Remind students that even if they disagree on some of the issues, they can write a single, unified letter with the use of phrases such as "Most of us believe . . ." or "While some of us think . . . ."

2. Ask students to write the top ten rules that should be followed in a classroom and the reason behind each rule. If students had to narrow the rules down to five, which would they keep? What if there could only be one school rule? What would be the best, single rule for a classroom?

3. Assign the writing of an essay on parenthood. Have students discuss rules that they intend to have for their children and how these rules differ or compare to the rules their parents have for them. Have them come up with consequences for broken rules.

Are U.S. Prisons Really Correctional Facilities?
By Duane Allen Ericson

Prisons, as we know them, have only existed for a century and a half. Primitive societies punished criminals through social disapproval, a demand for restitution to the victim, or—in extreme cases—exile from the tribe. Later, political states were more inclined toward corporal punishments including blinding, branding, cutting off hands, and executions.

Until the eighteenth century, confinement was only used for political prisoners and was often no more stringent than "house arrest." Following the Enlightenment—a time in history when politics, religion, and education all reflected a belief in the power of human reason—brutal punishments were abandoned in favor of making criminals "serve time" in prisons where they could be punished but also rehabilitated through discipline and moral instruction. However, a consistently high rate of repeat offenders has shattered the rehabilitation ideal.

Today, in America, a higher percentage of the population is incarcerated than in any other civilized country, at enormous—and growing—costs. Confinement of a single person averages $25,000 per year, and the prison population has tripled in the past two decades. Furthermore, overcrowding and the presence of gangs and violence inside prison walls thwart rehabilitation and tend to harden criminals who are likely never to escape a life of crime.

It is time we take a hard look at our prison system and its alternatives. We must also find ways to mend the fabric of our society, which today produces so much deviant behavior that close to half a percent of its citizens requires imprisonment. Bond issue "A," which would cost state tax payers $100 million dollars for new prisons, should be voted down. Building more prisons is not the answer.

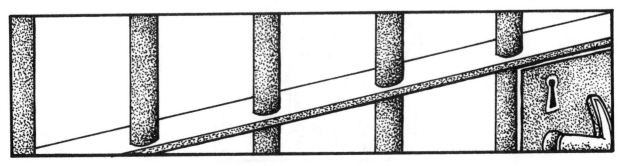

The Consequences of Crime

In many classrooms around America today, the consequences of misbehaving are appropriate to the behavior. A student who wastes a teacher's time may owe that teacher some of his or her own free time. A student who damages property may be asked to repair or pay for the damages. List five crimes that you frequently see reported on the news and an appropriate consequence for each crime. Do you think fewer crimes would be committed if criminals were required to pay restitution to victims and their families and to repair damages done during crimes?

Crime	Consequence
1.	
2.	
3.	
4.	
5.	

Punishment, Restitution, Rehabilitation, or Revenge?

The following are thought-provoking questions on the topic of prisons, which are not directly answered in the newspaper article by Mr. Ericson. Following a discussion of these questions with your group members, appoint a secretary to record your group's thoughts on a separate sheet of paper so that you will be prepared to share your answers with the entire class.

1. Even penologists and reformers disagree about the purpose of "punishing" a "crime." Is the purpose of punishment to deter others from criminal behavior, to take revenge, to reform a criminal, to lock away a dangerous person, or to prevent retaliation by victims?

2. In light of historical practices, should imprisonment be used for all forms of criminal behavior? When (if ever) might corporal punishment, restitution, or exile be more appropriate?

3. Nearly half of the prison population is confined for drug-related offenses, yet not even the government claims to be winning the war on drugs. Is there a better way to deal with such offenses?

4. What problems face a released prisoner who hopes to change his or her life to a lawful one?

5. The population of women prisoners is growing even faster than that of men, and the crimes they are committing are increasingly more violent. Why?

6. Australia was originally settled as a prison colony for Great Britain. Much of early America was made up of political prisoners, debtors, indentured servants, and fugitives from justice in other countries. Is a prison colony an option today? Why or why not?

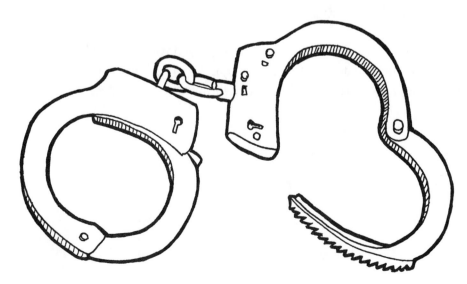

Genetic Genius

Background

There was a time when we knew very little about our insides. No one had seen a brain or a heart on x-ray, much less the remarkably small genes that determine so much of our personalities and our physical and mental make-up. Today, although scientists are not yet to the point of custom building blonde-haired, blue-eyed, intelligent little babies for picky couples, they can already inform future parents of their unborn child's genetically built-in defects. Soon, they will be able to tell any patient whether he or she is genetically inclined to contract cancer or another disease by a given age. Next, genetic engineering will be able to change one's genetic "problems."

Clearly, these amazing abilities carry the potential of both promise and disaster. Our technology is advancing at a pace our morality may have trouble keeping up with.

In this lesson, students form an opinion about the value of the continuing advancements in genetic research when they read a letter from a patient to her doctor set in the near future.

Understanding the Reading

1. Following a reading of Mrs. Brown's letter to her physician, students should be able to answer the following questions:

   a. Why did Mrs. Brown want her doctor to tell her about genetic tendencies she had toward various diseases? (She wanted to prepare herself and her family for what was to come. Other family members had died of cancer.)

   b. What reasons did Mrs. Brown give Doctor Godsey for changing her mind? (She feared her insurance company would raise her rates and/or her employer would "suggest" early retirement.)

   c. Do you think Mrs. Brown would have changed the way she lived her life had she found out she had a tendency toward cancer? (Perhaps she would have modified her diet and lifestyle, or perhaps she would have felt hopeless and depressed.)

Teaching Activities

1. Genetic counseling and engineering clearly carry with them both benefits and problems. Some suggest that our scientific knowledge is getting ahead of our moral/ethical maturity or that even the attempt to play with genes is really an attempt to play with fate or even "play God." Allow students to think about the pros and cons of genetic engineering with the "What's It Worth?" activity.

2. Even in the absence of genetic engineering, people pick up hints about their genetic make-up by noticing diseases that run in their families. Do people really alter their lives based on the probability of a tendency toward a given disease? Allow students to think critically about such questions by assigning the completion of the "Genetic Tendencies, Lifestyle Choices" activity.

Extensions

1. Assign students the writing and presentation of a three- to four-minute persuasive speech on either the need for or dangers of genetic counseling, research, or engineering.

2. Allow students to draw a picture and describe the perfect animal or the perfect plant by combining various aspects of real animals or plants.

3. Assign the completion of an essay on the pros and cons of "hand picking" a child's personality, appearance, athletic, and intellectual abilities.

Dear Dr. Godsey,

Please remove my name from the list of patients interested in discovering their genetic tendency toward cancer and other diseases which can be affected by diet and lifestyle choices. Although I appreciate your offering this service to your patients who desire the information, I must decline. Months ago, when I made the request, I was certain that this information would be helpful to me. My grandparents and both of my parents died of cancer, and I wanted to be able to prepare myself and my family for the hardships and sorrow that go along with that devastating disease. I even thought, since the procedure has become so simple, that I would like to know whether I had a genetic predisposition to any other lifestyle-related diseases while I was at it. I understand your position on the issue of informing patients of diseases they cannot prevent that will affect them in the future. I see the futility of learning something will happen to you that you cannot prevent.

I have decided to decline the genetic information about myself for two reasons. First of all, I am afraid that my insurance company will raise my rates should it discover I have a high probability toward cancer in my future. With computer technology being what it is, how can we not expect that our personal knowledge will soon be public knowledge? And once that happens, what will stop insurance companies from raising rates of high-risk customers? Worse yet, what will stop them from declining customers who are likely to experience medical problems in their future? In addition to this scare, I fear the company where I am employed will look for reasons to fire or retire me early should they, too, discover I have a tendency toward cancer.

Instead of putting the knowledge of a genetic tendency toward cancer on record, I will simply assume a lifestyle that presumes I have such a tendency. Shouldn't we all live life in as healthy a manner as possible regardless of what is in the cards for us genetically? Don't we owe that to our families and ourselves?

Sincerely,

Mrs. J. L. Brown

Mrs. J.L. Brown

What's It Worth?

Think of the potential benefits and problems of genetic counseling and engineering and fill out the chart below.

Genetic Counseling includes learning of existing birth defects in an unborn child, as well as learning of genetic tendencies toward diseases in the future of currently healthy individuals.

Potential Benefits

1. _____
2. _____
3. _____
4. _____
5. _____

Potential Problems

1. _____
2. _____
3. _____
4. _____
5. _____

Genetic Engineering is the idea that doctors may someday be able to dictate one's genetic make-up before his or her birth. Some liken this to "playing God" while others praise it as a means of preventing devastating diseases and defects. What is your opinion?

Potential Benefits

1. _____
2. _____
3. _____
4. _____
5. _____

Potential Problems

1. _____
2. _____
3. _____
4. _____
5. _____

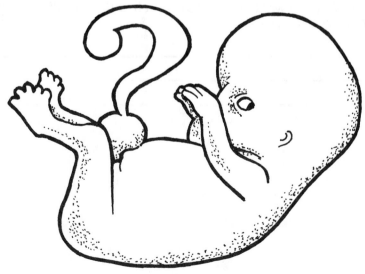

Genetic Tendencies, Lifestyle Choices

In pairs, think about, discuss, and write answers to the following questions on the subject of genetic research.

1. Even in the absence of genetic counseling, how do people pick up hints about their genetic make-up?

   _____

   _____

   _____

2. Are people likely to alter their lives in light of these hints? Why or why not?

   _____

   _____

   _____

3. How big of a role do you think lifestyle choices and other environmental issues play in regard to a person's health?

   _____

   _____

   _____

4. If you could know about your unborn child's personality, appearance, and other genetic traits before he or she was born, would you want to?

   _____

   _____

   _____

5. If he or she could, would you want your doctor to tell you about diseases you are likely to contract in your future? Why or why not?

   _____

   _____

   _____

Background

War is as old as human society itself. Economic, territorial, and identity conflicts continue to be responsible for the outbreak of fighting today.

Wars are fought with the best weapons available to a group of people. Sticks and stones progressed to spears and arrows, to longbows, catapults, gunpowder, naval warfare, air warfare, nitroglycerine, and finally nuclear bombs and even biological weapons.

Today the best weapons available to armed forces are so powerful that it is uncertain humanity can allow war to continue at all. At the peak of the Cold War, there were 50,000 nuclear warheads actively deployed—enough to exterminate all life seven times over. However, development of weapons for war has not been halted. Research continues in lasers that blind, particle beams that disable satellites and planes, suitcase nuclear bombs, unmanned aircraft, and computer viruses that could cripple economies and cause national chaos. It is certain that any positive scientific advancement will also yield potential for destruction. Human beings may have already reached a point in history where they must choose between living in peace or not surviving at all.

In this lesson, students read the diary entry of a teen-aged Civil War soldier and practice the skills of comparing and contrasting as they discuss the past, present, and future states of war.

Understanding the Reading

Following a reading of the teen's diary entry, students should be able to answer the following questions:

1. What things surprised and disappointed Tommy about the life of a soldier? (long marches, a uniform that did not fit, monotonous meals, lack of "action")

2. Why did Tommy question his desire to fight the Rebs near the end of his diary entry? (He had seen dead men and boys very much like himself.)

3. Why might Tommy have enlisted in the war? (He was bored with his life on the farm, wanted to see adventure, and wanted to stand up for his country.)

4. What rules are applied to wars of history and of today? (neutrality of medical personnel, humane treatment of prisoners, avoidance of direct assault on civilians)

Teaching Activities

1. The diary entry of the young teen talks of a war many years and many military advances ago. Lead a discussion about the similarities of war today and wars in the past. Also discuss the differences in past and present wars. What do students think wars of the future will be like? Will we ever get to a point where there are no wars on earth? Why or why not? In preparation for students making comparisons and contrasts about wars, require them to complete the "Quick Comparisons" activity, which gets them thinking about how to compare things that are familiar to them in their everyday lives.

2. Allow students to think critically about the meaning and essence of war. Divide students into groups of four or five and have them discuss and answer the questions in the "What Is War?" activity.

3. Although many veterans do not wish to discuss some specifics of their time spent on the battlefield, many are eager to share with others some of those experiences. Allow your students to get some inside knowledge of the life of a soldier by assigning them the completion of an interview with a veteran. Students may use the "Warrior Interview" activity to guide them in asking questions, or they may wish to formulate their own.

Extensions

1. Assign students the writing of a vivid, detailed account of their day describing both the day's events and their own feelings throughout the day. Ask students to compare and contrast their diary entries with Tommy's. What things differ because of the presence of war in Tommy's life? What things differ simply because of the times?

2. Read Jim Murphy's *The Boys War* (Scholastic Inc., New York, 1990).

3. Based on group discussions and the "What Is War?" findings, assign students to write a report about the future of war.

4. Assign the writing of a short story set in a society where there is no war, prejudice, hatred, or deceit.

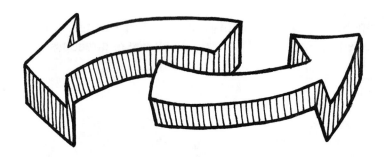

Quick Comparisons

1. You know you are in the big city when _____
   _____.

2. You know you are in a tiny town when _____
   _____.

3. You know you are in a fabulous restaurant when _____
   _____.

4. You know the restaurant is a dive when _____
   _____.

5. You know it is going to be a good day when _____
   _____.

6. You know it is going to be a bad day when _____
   _____.

7. You know you have got some growing up to do when you still _____
   _____.

8. You know you are getting old when _____
   _____.

9. You know you forgot to put your thinking cap on when _____
   _____.

10. You know you are having a smart day when _____
    _____.

August 17, 1862

Dear Diary,

I do not expect Johnny to come into my tent tonight and pour cold water on my feet. I expect the practical jokes have come to an end for all of us. They seemed to pass the time before today. It seemed we would do nothing but march and eat salt pork and beans, salt pork and beans day after day until now. When we stopped in Harper's Valley yesterday and added on yet another unit, it was as if we were a mile-long snake slithering on and on to nowhere to do nothing.

Endless marching is not what I expected when I signed on with the recruiter in town. Neither did I sneak away from the old farm and stand up straight so I could look 18 in the recruiter's office just to trade my farm clothes for a pair of too-long-legged trousers and a too-short-armed jacket. I was going to be outfitted in a fit uniform and marched right off into the middle of the Rebs where I would shoot my gun and come home a hero having shown them Southerners how to keep to their place.

Tonight I would just rather be milking the cows. I want a piece of Mother's apple pie. I want to sleep in my own bed with little brother, Sam, kicking at my feet. But instead it is time to truly go to war. We are so close now and I no longer feel any desire to fight anyone. For today, I had to step over dead men and boys no older than myself to continue on my march. We did not stop. Some of us seemed not even to look. Yet I could look at nothing else. Some men were so mangled as not to be recognizable by their mothers and others looked alive with their eyes open and their hands on their guns—but not moving at all, not breathing, not speaking, not looking ever again. And, somehow, it did not matter whether the dead men be Rebs or our own, though I would dare not say so to Johnny or any of the others. All that mattered was that these men would not be going home after the war. And tonight I lay and wonder if there ever will be an "after the war."

Fearful and unsure,
Tommy

What Is War?

Discuss the questions below with your group members. Appoint a secretary to record your group's responses on a separate sheet of paper. Be prepared to share your group's thoughts with the entire class.

1. If computer programs became so lifelike that they could imitate the human mind, what purposes of war might be dreamed up for them?

2. Give examples of sports, games, and play that are similar to fighting. In what ways are the games similar? What makes playing competitively and fighting a war different?

3. If there were no more war, would technology continue to advance?

4. Should scientists be blamed when their discoveries lead to weapons of war?

5. Can war be stopped? How?

6. The following technological achievements, improvements, and products were developed during or because of war. What were the military purposes of funding the development of the following?

    radar   submarines
    penicillin   jet planes
    rockets   telegraphs
    satellites   computers
    modern surgery

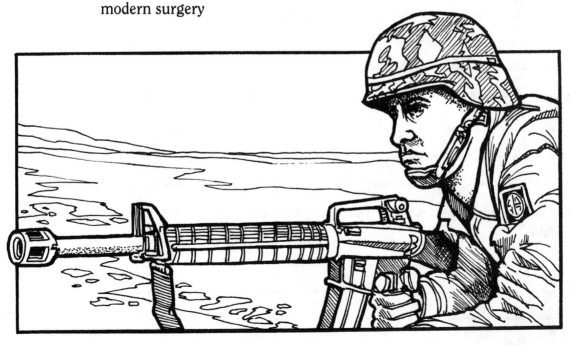

Warrior Interview

1. In which war did you serve? _____

2. In which of the armed forces did you serve? _____

3. Why did you join the armed forces?

   _____

   _____

4. What were your duties during wartime?

   _____

   _____

5. Describe a typical day during your wartime duty.

   _____

   _____

6. What things surprised you about the life of a soldier?

   _____

   _____

7. What are your feelings about war? Do you believe it is occasionally inevitable, or are there alternative ways for countries to solve conflicts?

   _____

   _____

   _____

8. In what ways has the experience of being a soldier changed or affected your life?

   _____

   _____

   _____

9. How do modern-day wars differ from those before the atomic bomb and other sophisticated weapons?

   _____

   _____

   _____

Background

Top names in entertainment today make as much as 10 to 12 million dollars every time they make a movie. The average free agent playing baseball for the Giants makes two million dollars a year. Meanwhile, the median family income in the United States stands at $33,000. The average factory worker, construction worker, and computer operator all average somewhere between ten to twenty-five dollars an hour.

Arguably, the distribution of wealth has not been equal in any country at any time. Even countries with overtly Communist ideals have admitted to bigger houses and fatter paychecks for their loyal officials than for their everyday man on the street. Yet if it can be assumed that big money goes to valued employment, then there has been a major shift in our country. We now value the athlete above the farmer, the movie star above the producer of foods and necessary goods.

In this lesson, students will think and write about the distribution of wealth in America. They will read an imaginary TV interview of people on the street and will write one of their own.

Understanding the Reading

Following a reading of the imaginary TV interview addressing the opinions of the public about the income of entertainers, students should be able to answer the following questions:

1. Why did Rebecca think entertainers were overpaid? (They left too little money for Rebecca and individuals like her.)

2. Why did Matt Peterson distinguish between athletes and entertainers before answering the Man on the Move's question? (He felt entertainers were overpaid, but professional athletes were not.)

3. How did self-interest play a role in both Rebecca's and Jenny's answers? (Rebecca wanted more money for herself and her family and felt she could have it if entertainers were not paid as much, and Jenny hoped to be a rich and famous movie star herself one day.)

Teaching Activities

1. Assign the "Important Employment" activity sheets and lead a class discussion on essential and nonessential jobs in America. Encourage library research in the completion of the column on page one of the activity which is set up to list the typical pay of various jobs.

Who Makes the Big Bucks in America?

2. CEOs in other industrialized countries make 20 to 30 times more than the average worker. In the United States, the average CEO makes 190 times as much as the workers in his or her company—another clear example of the unequal distribution of wealth in our country. Have students conduct an interview of schoolmates with the use of the "CEO Interview" page.

Extensions

1. The people who responded to the Man on the Move's questions in the interview supported their opinions with very few facts. Ask students to write an essay in answer to the same question the Man on the Move asked but to support their opinions with facts.

2. Following the interview of schoolmates, students may wish to graph the results of the "CEO Interview."

3. Assign students an essay in response to the question: "You have just won $10 million in the lottery. What are you going to do with the money?"

Important Employment—Page One

Think about the various jobs in America. Decide which of these jobs you consider essential and fill in the chart below. Use the library to assist you in finding the typical pay of the jobs you listed. Also list in the column provided what you consider to be the financial worth of each of the jobs you selected.

Jobs necessary to the survival of society	Job's Typical Pay	Job's Financial Worth
Jobs that help society		
Jobs that add to, but are not essential to, society		
Jobs that are not necessary to the survival of society		

Important Employment—Page Two

1. Look at the three jobs you listed as essential to the survival of society and answer the following questions:

   A. Do these jobs provide the basic necessities of food, clothing, and housing? _____
   _____

   B. Are these the highest paying jobs on the chart? _____

   C. Do you think they should be the highest paying jobs? _____

   D. Why or why not?_____
   _____

2. Now locate the four jobs on your chart which you consider to be the most difficult jobs. Circle them and then answer the following questions about the jobs you circled:

   A. What jobs did you circle? _____

   B. Are these the highest paying jobs? _____

   C. Do you think they should be? _____

   D. Why or why not?_____
   _____

3. Of all the jobs you listed, which is the highest paying? _____
   _____

4. Overall, do essential or nonessential jobs earn the highest wages? _____
   _____

5. How many jobs that you listed pay what you felt the job was worth? _____

6. What jobs on your list do you think should provide the highest income? Why? _____
   _____

7. What job traits would you consider to determine a job's financial worth? The job's necessity? Difficulty? Level of responsibility? Leadership requirements? Other? _____
   _____
   _____

CEO Interview

Discover what 20 of your schoolmates believe CEOs in America should be paid. Report to them the background information and ask them the questions that follow.

BACKGROUND INFORMATION: Chief Executive Officers are the head managers of large and prosperous companies. They are responsible for the entire operation of the business. The buck stops on the CEO's desk! Therefore, they are paid more than the other workers employed by the company.

QUESTION: How many times more than the average worker do you think CEOs make in America? _____

BACKGROUND INFORMATION: While CEOs in other major, industrialized countries make 20 to 30 times more than their companies' other employees, those in America make an average of 190 times more!

QUESTION: Do you think CEOs in America are paid too much? _____

QUESTION: Why or why not? _____

_____

Graph your results and/or discuss them with your classmates to see whether they got similar answers from the students they interviewed. Also discuss with your classmates how you would answer the questions asked in this interview.

"Good evening, ladies and gentlemen, I'm Channel Nine's Man on the Move and the question I ask of you, the general public, tonight is this: Do movie stars, sports stars, and other entertainers make too much money? Let's see what you think."

REBECCA JONES (grocery clerk): Heck, ya. Michael Jordan's hoggin' all the money, and that leaves enough for the store here to pay me only eight dollars an hour. I'm a single mom. I've got three kids to feed on that money!

MATT PETERSON (firefighter): The movie stars, yea, they get paid too much. They work on a movie for maybe two months and make a million dollars. But the athletes, now they work for it. They give their entire lives to their sport. They work out, eat right, and incur injuries that they have to live with for the rest of their lives. They have to move from city to city and have no say about their trades. They might get paid a lot, but they are retired by the age of 35.

JENNY HEFFELFINGER (college student): No way! Entertainers give us our sanity. This crazy world needs something to distract us from reality. I'm glad they make the big bucks. Their big houses and flashy cars are cool. I'm going to be a rich movie star myself. Maybe this Man on the Move interview will be my big break. What do you think?

NELLIE BOUCHAL (owner of national chain of women's clothing stores): There is no such thing as a person making too much money. People make what they want to make. If you want to make a lot of money, you don't settle for being a nurse's aide—you become a doctor. If you want to make a lot of money, you don't settle for bagging groceries—you open your own supermarket. Entertainers worked hard to get where they are to get the money they make. I came to this country with a 23-word English vocabulary and $65.00. You get what you work for.

Background

Advertising is as ancient as the marketplaces of the
earliest cities. Fishmongers, butchers, and traders used their
hoarse voices and bells to announce their presence—hardly unlike
the ice cream trucks still working neighborhoods today. Centuries later, with
the appearance of brand-name products, advertising took the forms with which we
are familiar today. Such products were promoted in newspapers and magazines, and later
on billboards, radio, and television. We now find advertisements on public buses, taxis,
and subways; on the backs of cash register receipts; under the windshield wipers of our
cars; in our sports stadiums, and above them on blimps in the sky; in our movie videos,
in our movies; in the paperback novels we read; and on the Internet we cruise.

Advertising has become a major intrusion into our daily lives, in addition to it being a
huge moneymaker. Media revenues, of which newspapers earn 29 percent, television 21
percent, and magazines 9 percent, are in excess of 170 billion dollars. Advertising is
tightly woven into the very fabric of American society. Has it become necessary to or
detrimental to the world we live in today?

In this lesson, students read an imaginary proposition for the banning of certain kinds of
advertisements and make personal judgments about the past, present, and future of
advertising. Because this is an imaginary proposal, students cannot truly read a statement
by the opposition, but they may write one as suggested in the first activity in the
"Extensions."

Understanding the Reading

Following a reading of the proposal for a proposition banning certain types of advertising,
students should be able to answer the following questions:

1. What do the supporters of Proposition 1872A mean by "intrusive advertising"?
   (advertising that interrupts a person's purpose or privacy)

2. What type of advertising would still be allowed under Proposition 1872A? (advertising
   necessary to the survival of a business, advertising that a consumer seeks)

3. What is an example of advertising that a consumer seeks out? (the Yellow Pages,
   catalogues that a consumer orders or buys)

4. How do television and radio ads interrupt a viewer's or listener's purpose? (The
   purpose is to watch a story or listen to music, not an ad.)

Teaching Activities

1. Divide students into groups of four or five so that they can have small group discussions about various forms of advertising. Assign the completion of the "What Do You Think" activity in directing students to consider critically such things as the following: If advertising were banned, who would pay for TV programs? Does political advertising make it harder or easier to select a candidate?

2. Proposition 1872A would need to be "advertised" itself if it were to pass an election. Perhaps its supporters would not mail out ads or put commercials on the radio or television, but they would need to do some nonintrusive advertising for the public to know what the proposition proposes. Ask students to pretend that it is their job to come up with a slogan and a drawing to send out to people who request information on Proposition 1872A. Have them write the slogan and draw the picture on the "Proposition 1872A—An End to Intrusive Advertising" activity sheet.

Extensions

1. Assign students the writing of an opposition statement to Proposition 1872A. What would be the arguments against banning various types of advertising?

2. Lead a class discussion on students' favorite and least favorite ads from TV, magazines, newspapers, billboards, and radio. Brainstorm what makes a popular ad, an unpopular ad, an honest ad, a dishonest ad.

3. Invite students to share stories (either oral or written) of times when advertisements have been intrusive in their lives (e.g., commercials interrupting a TV program, advertisements on the newspaper or magazine pages between the first page of a story and its conclusion, telemarketers calling at dinnertime)

4. Assign students the creation of ads either on paper or on video or audio cassette. Have students determine which ads are informative, which are persuasive, and which bend the truth or lie outright.

5. Write a company praising or complaining about its use of honest or dishonest advertising.

Advertising in America

Proposition 1872A states that all intrusive advertising be banned in the United States. Intrusive advertising includes all ads which infringe on a person's privacy by interrupting his or her purpose. Intrusive advertising does not include that advertising which is necessary to the survival of a business and/or that which a consumer seeks out for his or her own information.

Therefore, signs on buildings would not be banned under Proposition 1872A. Catalogues and shopping channels which a person intentionally reads or watches would not be banned under Proposition 1872A. Junk mail which one must thumb through to get to the letters and bills would be banned. Television and radio commercials which interrupt the program one intends to watch or listen to would be banned. Billboards which one does not set out on a trip to read would be banned under Proposition 1872A. Magazine and newspaper ads which one encounters in trying to finish an article that continues on another page would be banned.

Proposition 1872A makes sense for America. It would allow for the necessary advertising that promotes a business and informs its customers of its wares, while eliminating unwelcome intrusions into the private lives of the citizens of this nation.

This explanation of the purpose and intent of Proposition 1872A has been prepared and paid for by its authors, and is therefore biased to their point of view. Please read information from the opponents of this proposition before making a decision about your vote. An informed citizen makes an intelligent choice.

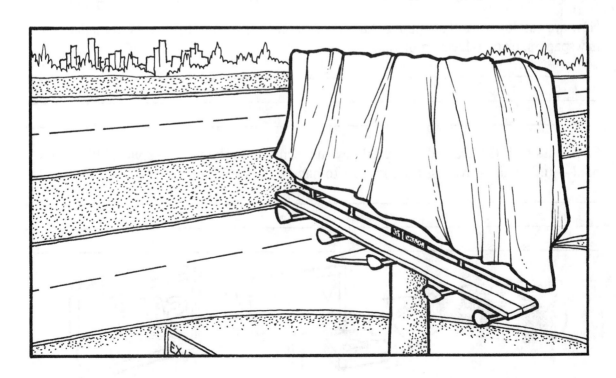

What Do You Think?

Discuss the following questions with the members of your group and record your responses on the lines provided. Use another sheet of paper if you run out of space. Be prepared to share your group's responses with the entire class.

1. If commercial advertising were banned—as cigarette advertising on TV and radio is now banned—how would television programs, radio, newspapers, and magazines be funded?

    _____

    _____

    _____

2. Although deceptive advertising is prohibited, it must be determined harmful to the consumer before the government will step in. Give examples of advertisements that bend the truth or even tell lies.

    _____

    _____

    _____

3. Does political advertising make it easier or harder for us to choose a good candidate?

    _____

    _____

    _____

4. How are catalogues and shopping channels different from advertisements in magazines and newspapers, or on television or radio?

    _____

    _____

    _____

5. First class mail (letters and packages) pays its own way in the postal service. Third class mail—junk mail—pays less than it costs to handle it. Is this fair?

    _____

    _____

    _____

Proposition 1872A—An End to Intrusive Advertising

Imagine that the supporters of Proposition 1872A have decided to send out no fliers and use no commercials on TV to get their message about intrusive advertising across. After all, they do not wish to use intrusive advertising themselves. However, they have decided to make a simple statement about the proposition available to any who might request it. Your job is to make a cover sheet for that simple statement. The cover sheet must include a slogan and a drawing. Create your cover sheet here.

Government Growth

Background

In primitive tribes, a strong set of traditions enforced by communal opinion constitutes government. Modern westerners find this simplicity perplexing, accustomed as they are to laws backed by police forces and judiciaries. One tribal chief, criticized for not ordering his people to follow his decision, replied in explanation, "If I told my people what to do, I would not be chief." In the same manner, Gandhi has been quoted as saying, "There go my people—I must hurry and catch up with them, for I am their leader!"

Such diffuse authority functions well in a society of fewer than 100 members, but as nation-states developed, so did the institutions of centralized government. Whether a monarchy, an aristocracy, or a republic, it is clear in a political state who makes decisions and how they will be enforced. And although such formalized institutions are necessary, there is a strong feeling today that government is far too intrusive in America.

In this lesson, students examine the purpose of government and form an opinion about what might be the ideal level of government involvement when they read a mock letter from a modern-day citizen to the Founding Fathers of America.

Understanding the Reading

Following a reading of the letter from the modern citizen to the Founding Fathers, students should be able to answer the following questions:

1. What is the main purpose of any government? (to collect taxes to provide for a common defense, and to state and uphold the laws of the land)

2. What is the modern citizen's main complaint against today's government? (It has gotten too big. Regulatory bodies oversee so many facets of life that red tape overtakes citizens' lives.)

3. With the establishment of what commission did the great growth of government begin, according to the author of this letter? (with the establishment of the Interstate Commerce Commission and the other regulatory bodies that followed it)

Teaching Activities

1. Assign the "A Day in My Life" activity. Remind students as they write about how government impacts their lives from morning to night that there are many minor ways government is involved that they probably do not think about consciously. For example, a government regulatory body decided just what must be included on the label of the cereal box they pour cereal from in the morning.

2. Require students to think critically about what the government is for by completing the "Who Needs Rules, Anyway?" activity in groups of three or four. Ask them to consider why anarchism would or would not work in a school, a family, or an entire society.

Extensions

1. Assign a report on various forms of government, various regulatory bodies, or on students' own opinions concerning how involved a government should be in the everyday lives of its citizens.

2. Establish a classroom government to organize a spirit week and other class activities and to enforce class rules. Choose new representatives periodically.

3. Use E-mail to write to students from countries with other forms of government. Find out how government impacts the lives of children in other countries.

4. Research the American Indian Society and its form of government.

Dear Founding Fathers,

I'm writing to let you know just what has become of the democracy you created when this fine country was founded. Of course, the presence of some sort of government body was essential to the establishment of a new nation. Every society of people since the beginning of time has had some form of government. Even social animals—lions, wolves, and baboons—develop some hierarchy of authority. And democracy was an excellent choice. As you expected, it has allowed for the collection of taxes to provide for a common defense while making possible continuous revision of laws, rights, and responsibilities in the changing times. What might surprise you is the phenomenal number of people the government requires to accomplish these goals today.

I suppose it all began in 1887 with the establishment of the Interstate Commerce Commission, a regulatory body overseeing the railroad, which was fast becoming the nation's largest employer and its most powerful business. In the 1920s, when the nation experienced an economic collapse now called the Great Depression, more regulatory bodies were created: the FCC, the SEC, the FDA, the NLRB, the WPA, and the TVA. Today, regulatory bodies oversee more facets of life than you might imagine. Each regulatory body, considered in and of itself, serves a necessary purpose, but together they constitute a monster.

In America today, more people work in government than in all manufacturing jobs combined. That means there are more people regulating the production of things than there are people producing things!

We have a name for the mess. We call it "red tape." Everyone knows about it. No one likes it. We all put up with it. Tell me, Founding Fathers of America, is this anything like you envisioned? And if not, how do we slow down, back up, and return to the place you started where the people are in control of the government and not the other way around?

A Modern Citizen

42

A Day in My Life

Think about the activities in which you are involved and how the government impacts each of those activities. Then, fill in the chart below by listing the activities that might be included in a typical day in your life. Remember in filling out the Government Impact column that the government affects you in ways you seldom think about. Two example activities have been completed for you.

Time	Activity	Government Impact
6:30 a.m.	Awakened by alarm clock made in China	Determined trading laws in China
7:00 a.m.	Ate cereal with milk	Created food preparation and packaging laws

Who Needs Rules, Anyway?

Discuss the following questions with the members of your group and record your responses below. Use another sheet of paper if you run out of space. Be prepared to share your group's responses with the entire class.

1. In the late nineteenth century in Eastern Europe, the movement of *anarchism* grew rapidly and met with some practical success. Anarchists believe people can live without institutions of authority, and they reject all government forms including capitalism and communism. Would it work to have no rules at school? At home? In the entire nation? Why or why not?

   _____

   _____

   _____

2. Who constitutes the government at school? What are the functions of these people? Without these people, how would these functions be accomplished?

   _____

   _____

   _____

3. If the government cut its number of employees in half, what kinds of work might the former government employees do that might be more productive?

   _____

   _____

   _____

4. Why is "providing for the common defense" the first order of business for most governments?

   _____

   _____

   _____

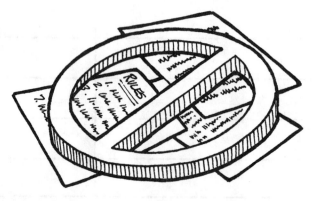

Background

Every civilized society has had some legal means of deciding when and if a buyer has been cheated when it comes to consumer products, yet only in this century has the seller of a product been held legally responsible for actual injuries caused to the buyer. This new legal concept places the burden of being certain a product will work as promised, will not cause harm if used correctly, and will carry warnings to prevent incorrect use that might hurt someone on the manufacturer and the seller.

In this lesson, students study consumer product safety goals when they read a letter to an imaginary columnist and his response.

Understanding the Reading

Following a reading of the Nelson Know-It-All letter and response, students should be able to answer the following questions:

1. Why are warning labels placed on the packaging of many consumer products? (to warn consumers about potential hazards of misuse of the product)

2. In what ways are the maker and seller of products responsible for their safety and effectiveness? (Products must be thoroughly tested for safety and effectiveness, government regulatory bodies determine rules to which makers and sellers must adhere, and consumers can sue manufacturers and retailers for injuries.)

3. Why were such stringent consumer product safety laws not necessary a century ago? (The range of available products was limited, new products were rare, and the proper use of existing products was common knowledge.)

Teaching Activities

1. Warning labels are all around us—so much so, in fact, that we often ignore them. Require students to take notice of warning labels found around the home and school by completing the "Warning Label Hunt" activity. Which warning labels make sense and which really go too far?

2. Allow students to write their own warning labels for products commonly used at school by assigning the completion of the "Warning: May Cause Serious Learning to Take Place" activity.

3. Some have suggested we have become a sue-happy nation. Allow students to think critically about the issue. Divide students into groups of three or four and assign the completion of the "Critical Thinking About Consumer Product Safety" activity.

Extensions

1. Assign students the completion of library research comparing auto accident injury/deaths prior to and after the introduction of seatbelts.

2. Assign research on the muckrakers, the Progressive Era, Upton Sinclair, Theodore Roosevelt, the Pure Food and Drug Act of 1906, Ralph Nader, or other eras and/or individuals concerned about consumer safety and fairness.

3. A boy who is seriously injured while in-line skating sues the manufacturer because, although written warnings advised the use of helmet and protective clothing, a picture on the instructional booklet showed a skater not wearing a helmet. Hold a mock trial with the defendant and attorneys.

NELSON KNOW-IT-ALL'S MAILBAG

Dear Nelson Know-It-All,

Why do so many labels have written warnings about the proper use of the product inside?

Signed, Nosy Ned

Well Nosy,

Until very recently in history, the policy of *caveat emptor*—a Latin phrase meaning "let the buyer beware"—prevailed as far as product safety was concerned. The range of available products was very limited and new products were rare. People grew up knowing not to stand behind a mule, not to eat meat that smelled bad, and not to play with fire. But the explosive growth in consumer goods during the last hundred years has meant new and unfamiliar dangers. Misusing products can cause tragic results. New products arrive in stores so frequently that if people had to figure out for themselves how *not* to use them, our emergency rooms would be full to capacity. A much better way is to make the maker or seller of the product test it for potential hazards and then put warnings on the label.

Warning labels are just one way consumers are made safe today. Federal agencies such as the Food and Drug Administration and the Consumer Product Safety Commission set rules that protect customers from unreasonable risks in what they buy. Many people also depend on the evaluation of new products provided by private organizations such as Consumers Union, the organization that publishes *Consumer Reports*. And, of course, a very effective means of assuring safety is found in the courts. Consumers can sue manufacturers and retailers, either individually or in a "class action" suit and win compensation for injuries.

So, the warning labels may seem excessive, Nosy, but they are there as a protection for you and your friends when you buy a new product and are uncertain about its safe and proper use. Thanks for your question.

Sincerely,
Nelson Know-It-All

Warning Label Hunt

Look around your home and find ten labels that give written warnings to the consumer about what not to do with a product (e.g., do not use a hair dryer in a bathtub, do not take with alcohol, etc.). You will find that some warnings make sense, while others are a bit far-fetched because the average consumer would never be expected to use a product in such a way suggested. Write the ten warnings you found below and indicate whether they are sensible or far-fetched. Try to find at least one label you find ridiculous.

Warning 1:

Warning 6:

Warning 2:

Warning 7:

Warning 3:

Warning 8:

Warning 4:

Warning 9:

Warning 5:

Warning 10:

Warning: May Cause Serious Learning to Take Place

Imagine you are the manufacturer of school products. Write warning labels for the following products to students and teachers:

Yellow #2 Pencils Warning:	Student Desk and Chair Warning:
8th Grade Science Book Warning:	Yellow, Dust-free Chalk Warning:
Compass and Protractor Set Warning:	Lined, Recycled Paper Warning:
Green, Plastic Lunch Trays Warning:	White, All-purpose Glue Warning:

Critical Thinking About Consumer Product Safety

Discuss the questions below with your group members. Appoint a secretary to record your group's responses on a separate sheet of paper. Be prepared to share your group's thoughts with the entire class.

1. Consumers have been known to sue businesses and manufacturers for injuries incurred from mistakes that might be considered the consumer's own fault (spilling coffee on oneself, cutting oneself on a window when trying to escape a home one has just robbed, etc.). Is there a point where the right to sue is taken too far?

2. If it were carried to the ridiculous, what other features of modern life might be required to carry disclaimers or warning labels (e.g., weather reports, political commercials)? Give an example of a possible law suit that might follow a weather report that failed to provide a disclaimer.

3. Should you be able to sue a company for false advertising? Why or why not?

4. Should you be able to sue a politician for breaking campaign promises? Why or why not?

Background

Marketplaces sprang up in Middle Eastern cities four to five thousand years ago wherein vendors peddled items from artisans and traders. With the passing of time, the booths and stalls of the marketplace became the storefronts of modern downtown areas. Until this century such stores were usually specialized and family owned and operated.

Retail sales began to change dramatically in the late nineteenth century with the arrival of the department store. By the 1920s the independent shop owner was also threatened by the rapid growth of chain stores and self-service supermarkets. These new kinds of retail operations were able to turn greater volumes of goods at lower prices and were so successful that laws were passed to protect the survival of the independent retailer.

With the growth of the suburbs after World War II and the highway construction that expanded mobility by car, the shopping center and franchise stores evolved as well. In addition to these forms of sales, retailers today also rely on mail order, multi-level marketing out of the home, home shopping channels on television, and shopping by computer. These forms of sales provide low overhead and high accessibility and are likely to challenge the success of the enormous discount houses found in today's shopping malls.

In this lesson, students are walked through the computer-screen sale of a broom and are asked to make judgments about the advantages and disadvantages of virtual shopping as well as other ways to purchase goods.

Understanding the Reading

Following a reading of the computer-shopper interaction, students should be able to answer the following questions:

1. When might a shopper opt for the "browse the entire mall" choice? (when shopping for a gift and having no specific idea in mind, when wanting to be updated on the network's choices in "stores," etc.)

2. What are the advantages and disadvantages of shopping by computer?
   (Advantages
   1. you never have to leave home
   2. someone has already researched product's quality
   3. someone has already done price comparison.
   Disadvantages
   1. you do not see, touch, or try out the actual item yourself
   2. you must wait for your merchandise to be delivered
   3. you have no chance to pick up something else off the shelf that you may have also been looking for as you might in a store.)

3. What seem to be the costs for the retailers using the network versus overhead for the owner of a store? (Network retailer—data entry workers to update information, employees to process purchase orders, employees to deliver goods. Store owner—rental of space, clerks, janitors, employees to stock shelves, employees to order goods.)

Teaching Activities

1. Individuals shop at various places because of the convenience of the location, price of its products, quality of its products, and other factors. Allow students to think critically about the pros and cons of various methods of shopping by completing the "Christmas Shopping" activity.

2. Does today's demand for lower prices and readily available products mean products today are of less quality and/or durability than products of the past? Require students to think of at least five items that just are not what they once were with the use of the "Quality Decline" activity.

3. Ask students to consider how shoppers bought food before there were supermarkets, whether they would rather stay in a bed and breakfast or a national chain hotel, and other consumer questions by assigning the completion of the "Retail Shopping Alternatives" activity.

Extensions

1. Create a class store where pencils, pens, stickers, and other items can be purchased with money received for good behavior or model citizenship.

2. Ask students to write a brief ad for an item they bring from home. Create a Home Shopping Program by videotaping students advertising their products.

3. Assign an essay detailing how room service, home delivery of foods, and other services have led to the home shopping channels of today and could lead to a time in the future when consumers never need to leave their homes. Require students to consider what this will mean to our social skills and our very way of life.

Good Evening! You have reached the E-mail address of Shopping on the Network. Please highlight one of the following:

BROWSE THE ENTIRE MALL

LOCATE ALL STORES IN ONE CATEGORY

[LOCATE A SPECIFIC ITEM]

You have chosen to locate a specific item. Please type in the name of the item selected:

BROOM

There are 37 brooms listed in the Shopping on the Network system. How would you like them listed?

[ALPHABETICAL BY MANUFACTURER'S NAME]

QUALITY RATING—HIGHEST TO LOWEST RATING

PRICE RATING—LEAST TO MOST EXPENSIVE

You have selected the alphabetical listing of brooms. Highlight the broom you would like to learn more about.

ATLANTA BRUSH AND BROOM

BOZO'S BROOMS

[CLEVELAND CLEANER]

You have highlighted the Cleveland Cleaner. The Cleveland Cleaner is a wooden-handled, straw-bristled broom suitable for indoor or outdoor use. It has a durability rating of three years and an overall quality rating of six on a scale from one to ten. The Cleveland Cleaner's list price is $9.52. It is in the mid-price range of brooms listed on the Shopping on the Network system. Would you like to purchase the Cleveland Cleaner?

[YES]

NO

You have indicated your interest in purchasing the Cleveland Cleaner. Please type in your name, phone number, E-mail address, physical address, and credit card number. Press the number sign to print out your warranty and a Cleveland Cleaner coupon. Your Cleveland Cleaner will arrive at your home in three to four days. Thank you for shopping on the Shopping on the Network system.

Christmas Shopping

List the pros and cons of the various types of stores and methods of Christmas shopping listed below.

Type of Store/Shopping Method	Pros	Cons
Department Store		
Shopping Mall		
Older Downtown Area		
Discount Warehouse		
Mail-order Catalog		
Home Shopping Channels		
Computer Network		

Quality Decline

With consumers today demanding merchandise at lower prices, manufacturers have been forced to lower their products' quality and durability in many cases. Ask your parents to help you list at least five products that have declined in quality/durability during the past few years. Be prepared to discuss your findings with your classmates. Three have been done for you.

Product	How Quality Has Declined
Candy bar	Smaller, fewer nuts and "extras"
Automobile	Less steel, less horsepower, more expensive to repair
Furniture	Pressed wood and plastic replaced metal and wood

CANDY

Retail Shopping Alternatives

Consider the following questions and record your opinions in the spaces provided.

1. Until the supermarket appeared, food shopping meant going into a market and having the proprietor retrieve from behind the counter each item you had chosen. Then you would go to the butcher and finally stop at the produce or farmers' market. Today, no one asks a salesclerk to get items from behind the counter, but butcher shops and farmers' markets are still popular. Why?

   _____

   _____

   _____

   _____

2. If prices were equivalent, would you rather stay at a bed and breakfast or a national chain hotel? Would you prefer to eat at a family-owned restaurant or a restaurant that is part of a national chain? Would you rather buy clothes at a discount department store or a small shop that tailors to the individual? Why?

   _____

   _____

   _____

   _____

3. Do the mass production and sales of a product necessarily lower its quality? Why or why not?

   _____

   _____

   _____

   _____

4. Which would you rather *work* in: a department store, a shopping mall store, an older downtown store, a discount warehouse, or a catalog mail-order company? Why?

   _____

   _____

   _____

   _____

56

Background

The United States Constitution guarantees accused
parties in both civil and criminal cases the right to a trial
by jury. This right we take for granted. Yet, except for Canada and
Great Britain, most countries have justice systems that allow jury trials
only in special circumstances or not at all.

The American Justice System

The concept of empanelling a group of the defendant's peers to weigh evidence against
him or her and decide guilt or innocence is an old one. Anglo-Saxon law as early as A.D.
900 gathered witnesses and acquaintances to conduct inquiries in legal disputes. But it
was the French, in their conquest of England in 1066, who introduced jury trials (as we
know them) and later codified them in English common law in the twelfth century.
English common law spread to its colonies, including America, and denial of that right to
trial by jury was one of the complaints listed by the Founding Fathers in the Declaration
of Independence.

Today the concept of trial by jury, as it has been applied in the United States, has been
called into public discussion by sensationalized trials, convictions overturned by
technicalities, and various other abuses of the system.

In this lesson, students read an argument presented to a panel of jurors in favor of the
American justice system and make a personal judgment about the fairness of our legal
system today. Students also research and define many legal terms and conduct a mock
trial.

Understanding the Reading

Following a reading of the lawyer's speech to the jury, students should be able to answer
the following questions:

1. What are some of the things this lawyer cites in suggesting that today's justice
   system itself is on trial? (multi-million dollar product liability suits, sensationalized
   criminal cases, questionable defenses, and the fact that big-time lawyers seem to be
   able to argue the rich and famous to their innocence)

2. How have some states attempted to reform their justice systems? (Some have
   reduced the size of their juries; others have made possible certain convictions on less
   than unanimous verdicts.)

3. What does this lawyer suggest must be done before the justice system can undergo
   meaningful reform? (The American public needs to agree on just what justice
   means.)

Teaching Activities

1. Before the use of the jury system, trials were often decided by ordeal. Allow students to develop a complete essay giving their opinion of justice by ordeal, or, as an alternative, allow them to discuss the idea of "double jeopardy" in an essay format by assigning the "And Justice for All" activity.

2. Several steps lead to a jury trial in the United States. Assign students the investigation into these various steps as they complete "The Trial Trail" activity.

Extensions

1. Ask students to research how military courts differ from civil and criminal courts.

2. Have students arrest you for giving exams that are too difficult. Choose a defense attorney and have the class select a prosecutor and a jury. Conduct a mock trial.

3. Statistics show that minorities are much more likely to be judged guilty in trials and to draw more severe sentences. Ask students to research this phenomenon in another country or another time period (e.g., Jews in Czarist Russia, early Christians in Roman times, American Communists or Socialists in the 1950s).

Ladies and Gentlemen of the Jury,

Today the American justice system itself is on trial. It is not you, the jury, that is in question. The jury system itself is a sound one providing for fair verdicts. It is the sideshows of the justice system that we must reform.

Highly publicized recent trials have called into question the justice system in America, and rightly so. Multi-million dollar product liability awards, sensational criminal cases that are on television, and criminal defenses based on questionable "excuses" such as the Twinkie defense (excessive dependence on junk food) and the post-traumatic stress syndrome have made all of us impatient with the justice system.

It is time for a change. Eighty percent of all jury trials worldwide take place in the United States. We claim two thirds of the world's lawyers. Yet criminals seem to have more rights than victims do, convictions are overturned on technicalities, the appeals process seems to go on forever, and acquittals can be bought with enough money for a good lawyer.

There must be another way, a better way, a revised way to handle our disputes. Some states have tried. They have reduced the size of their juries from twelve to six people and have made possible certain convictions on less than unanimous verdicts. But the justice system continues to bring outrageous results. It is time we condemn it like an old, dilapidated building and build a solid structure in its place. Ladies and gentlemen of the jury, I ask you to convict the Twinkie defense and the ability to buy freedom in the form of an exceptionally clever lawyer. I ask you to find our current justice system guilty of becoming a three-ring circus. And, in addition, I ask you to work with all Americans to come up with a clear agreement on what justice really looks like so we can begin the rebuilding of a good idea gone bad—justice by jury.

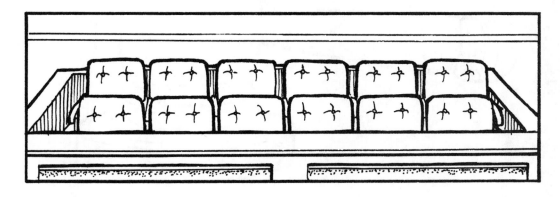

And Justice for All

Choose one of the questions below and respond to it on a separate sheet of paper. Develop a complete essay for your answer. Be certain your essay states your opinion, lists supporting points, and ends with a strong conclusion. Your essay should be two to four paragraphs long.

1. Before use of the jury system, trials were often decided "by ordeal." The accused might have to carry a pound of red-hot iron for a distance with bare hands, or be bound and dropped into a river. If the accused's hands were burned or the body floated, the judgment was "guilty." In some disputes, the opposing parties had to fight to see who God would allow to win. By A.D. 1215, the accused could avoid trial by ordeal by paying a small sum for a jury trial. If you were guilty, which choice would you make and why? What if you were innocent? Explain why people believed "ordeals" to be fair.

2. In the United States, "double jeopardy" is forbidden. That means that once acquitted, a person can never again be charged for an alleged crime, even if he or she afterwards confesses publicly. Is this fair? Suppose a teacher could demand you retake a test you had already passed. Suppose once you got a driver's license you never had to be tested again. Why are these cases different, or are they?

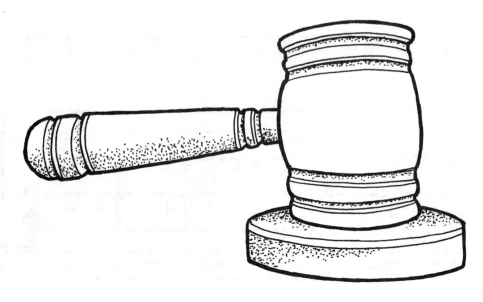

The Trial Trail

Several steps lead up to a jury trial in the United States justice system. This process takes so long that it is argued that the constitutional right to a speedy trial is being violated. Going through the process, with all its legal expenses, is a serious punishment in and of itself—for the innocent as well as the guilty. Are there steps that could be eliminated? With the use of a dictionary, encyclopedia, or more extensive library research, define the following steps.

STEP	DEFINITION
1. Arrest	_____ _____ _____
2. Arraignment	_____ _____ _____
3. Bail	_____ _____ _____
4. Preliminary hearing	_____ _____ _____
5. Grand jury indictment	_____ _____ _____
6. Pre-trial procedures	_____ _____ _____
7. Plea bargaining	_____ _____ _____
8. Jury trial	_____ _____ _____

Labor Unions

Background

Modern-day labor unions evolved gradually from the guilds found in Europe nearly 2,000 years ago. Guilds composed of craftsmen in a particular occupation set professional standards and wages and functioned almost as a quasi-government in their towns. They were responsible for taking care of sick members, policing, educating, regulating trade, and supporting the arts and the church.

Guild influence waned with the emergence of capitalism during the Renaissance and the explosion of trade. During Napoleon's reign over Europe, guilds were abolished.

With the Industrial Revolution came the concept of labor as a commodity, and by the late nineteenth century, labor unions were blossoming in England, America, France, and Germany. Although there was a period in the nineteenth century (1830-1885) when unions struggled to reform capitalistic society toward more utopian goals, unions have for the most part cooperated with capitalism's view of worker as commodity by banding together to "sell" their labor.

Union membership in America has been primarily concentrated in factories, mines, and transportation. As these industries have become mechanized and the economy has shifted toward service and financial industries, the only significant recent growth in union membership has been among government workers. Only a little over ten percent of the work force now belongs to unions. It is generally agreed that this is a large factor in the stagnation of middle-class earnings during the past three decades.

Understanding the Reading

Following a reading of the union president's speech, students should be able to answer the following questions:

1. Why does the new union president believe unions are essential in a capitalistic society? (He believes capitalism is based on greed and unions act as a kind of check-and-balance.)

2. What reason does the new union president give for the recent decline in labor union enrollment? (He believes it is harder to organize computer operators and telemarketers than people who build things in factories.)

Teaching Activities

1. Labor unions have pros and cons. Can effective economy grow without labor unions? Can it be good for humanity as a whole to have owners and workers opposing each other? Allow students to think critically, considering the various aspects of labor unions, by assigning the completion of the "Solidarity—Does It Work?" activity.

2. Labor unions have been responsible for such social laws as child labor laws and regulations on safety in the workplace. Require students to research such laws with the use of the "Labor Laws" activity.

Extension

1. Assign the writing of reports on societies which do not hold profit and growth as primary goals. Such societies include the Eskimos, Native Americans, and Bushmen.

2. Have students band together to request something from the principal and school board that would enhance the school without distracting from education or costing too much money (establishment of a student council, the planting of a school garden).

Union brothers and sisters, thank you for electing me president of the great AFL-CIO! Your overwhelming support tells me—and this whole country—that it's time for labor unions to rally and change. From this day forward we'll be heading in some new directions, the directions we talked about all through this campaign. Lately, the media has been writing obituaries for the labor movement in America. They say times have changed and unions are obsolete. Let me reply here and now: as long as capitalism is around, unions will be strong! Capitalism means owners hungry for profits who do not care about anything except profits. That kind of greed was kept in check by the government and the church until the Renaissance in Europe 600 years ago. Then, when the Industrial Revolution came along, things got even worse for workers, and they had to organize against the owners—against Standard Oil and Carnegie Steel and the railroad barons. In other words, corporate capitalism! They united to fight for better working conditions and better pay. That's what we call "bread and butter" unionism, and it's the reason America was the first country in the history of the world to have a broad middle class. Through their organizing, their solidarity, and their strikes, unions *created* the middle class! Now that middle class is in trouble because factories are being moved overseas for cheap labor, the good jobs left are going to computers. Union membership has dropped from 25 percent to 10 percent because it is a lot harder to organize computer programmers and medical insurance office managers and remote telemarketing operators than it is people who make things with their hands who are in close proximity with their fellow workers. But we can do it! And do you know why? Because Silicon Valley is capitalism and HMOs are capitalism and investment firms are capitalism! And as long as you've got that kind of greed running things, you need unions! Solidarity forever!

Thank you!

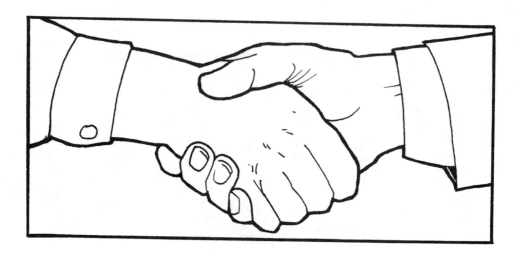

Solidarity—Does It Work?

Critically consider the pros and cons of labor unions and answer the questions below. Remember, they are opinion questions. They do not have one single correct answer, but your opinion needs to be supported by facts, anecdotes, and/or statistics.

1. Most of the growth in union membership in the last three decades has been among government employees. Such unions, however, do not—as a rule—have the right to call a strike. Why is this so? What are the pros and cons of this rule?

   _____

   _____

   _____

   _____

2. Many people believe that when a union is powerful, efficiency in the industry is increased, leading to lower prices of its products and services even though wages go up. Why might this happen?

   _____

   _____

   _____

   _____

3. When owners and workers oppose each other, is it good for humanity as a whole? Who looks out for the environment? Consider the case of the lumber companies and the loggers; does either side have an interest in the long-range value of the forest?

   _____

   _____

   _____

   _____

4. Is it possible to have a healthy and effective economy in which profit and growth are not the primary goals?

   _____

   _____

   _____

   _____

Labor Laws

Labor unions have been directly responsible for much social legislation including child labor laws, safety and health regulations in the workplace, and medical coverage and pension plans for workers. Use the library to research these areas, and record below three laws that pertain to each area. How must work have been different before the establishment of these laws? Who will enforce and expand on these laws should labor unions die?

Child Labor Laws

The Law	The Date Established
1. _____	_____
2. _____	_____
3. _____	_____

Safety and Health Regulations in the Workplace

The Law	The Date Established
1. _____	_____
2. _____	_____
3. _____	_____

Medical Coverage and Pension Plans for Workers

The Law	The Date Established
1. _____	_____
2. _____	_____
3. _____	_____

Background

In her anthropological studies, Margaret Mead noticed three types of cultures: those in which children learn from their elders and ancestors, those in which children learn from their peers, and those in which parents learn from their children.

As early as 1970 she saw America evolving into the third type of culture. By that time the country was already changing so quickly that the values and skills of adults were obsolete. Not being able to see what a future adult would need to be, children had no role models and did not even define adulthood until they themselves reached it.

Margaret Mead was not the only one to notice the change. Booksellers, movie producers, politicians, advertisers, and even parents themselves began to alter their traditional ways, emphasizing the needs of children over those of parents. Today we are a society that caters to children because the future that is theirs is already arriving, before they are grown.

Yet as we encourage them to be mini-adults, we deny them any true childhood. Unstructured and imaginative playtime has turned into a series of structured "events." Innocence once protected is now exposed to explicit images of sex and violence. Teenagers are tried in adult courts and sent to adult prisons. Overworked parents in crises unburden financial, romantic, and social problems on their children. Young children are taught the use of 911 and then left home alone for hours each day after school.

In this lesson, students make judgments about what it means to be a child in America today. They discuss the three types of culture Margaret Mead observed and make predictions about America in the future.

Understanding the Reading

Students should be able to answer the following questions after reading the letter from the 11-year-old boy to his mother.

1. In some ways Mark has already entered the adult world at age 11. List some of the things he talks about that prove it. (feeding the dog, washing the dishes, helping his mother figure out the new computer setup)

2. What are some signs that Mark is still very much a kid? (his mom and dad taxi him to ballgames, he is planning a birthday party at his dad's, he has to complete his homework and study for tests)

3. Is Mark's childhood similar to others his age in America today? (Answers will vary. Students may compare Mark to others they know who have divorced parents, are home alone after school, know more about computers than the teacher, etc.)

Teaching Activities

1. Adults who know that their children are entering a future much more complicated than the world of yesterday, or even today, sometimes cater to their children to give them as many advantages as possible and sometimes treat their children as mini-adults. Ask students to think about such situations as they are listed on the "I Am the Future" activity.

2. Margaret Mead suggested that America is a prefigurative society in which children teach their parents. Have students indicate what things they know more about than their parents with the "Prefigurative Cultures" activity.

3. Margaret Mead noted three types of cultures around the world: Postfigurative, Prefigurative, and Configurative. Allow students to study each with the use of the "Answers from Anthropology" activity.

Extensions

1. Assign students the research of the treatment of children in different countries and during different times in history. How are schools different in Japan? Do children treat adults differently in China? Students may wish to study the industrial world before child labor laws or the place of children in nonindustrial societies today. Are there differences in the way girls and boys are treated in the various cultures?

2. Ask students to research individuals who have studied child development or who have stood up for children throughout history. They may also wish to learn about great teachers throughout history.

3. Allow students to work with younger students by setting up E-mail pen pals at an elementary school or some other buddy system where kids work together periodically or on one big project.

4. Allow students to read about the field of anthropology or about Margaret Mead. Students may wish to report their findings to the class.

Dear Mom,

I've finished my homework, fed the dog, and washed the dishes and I am tired so I'm going to bed early. I hope you had a good day at work. Did Mr. Nelson talk to you again at lunch today? I really think you should go out with him. Oh, Dad called and said to remind you he's picking me up Friday night for the ballgame on Saturday. I'll be home on Sunday after Grandma's. And Jeff's mom wants to know if we can drive Jeff to karate Tuesday night. She has to work late.

I watched a cool movie on the family channel tonight. I wish you could have seen it with me and didn't have to work overtime again. Anyway, there was this commercial on for this rock CD collection—very retro. Wouldn't mind that for my birthday next month. Can you believe I'm going to be 12, Mom? Don't worry about a party. Dad's having all the guys over to his house. Supposed to be a surprise but Ryan already told me.

School was okay. I had to show Mr. Mason how to multi-task the software. It takes him so long to look things up in the manual that some kid always figures things out just messing around before he can. Jack spent the entire period in the computer lab writing messages to some girl in Pennsylvania and Mr. Mason never caught on. We were supposed to be searching databases on the Internet for information on our science projects. Did you figure out how to download the graphics from your hard drive at work yet? I could show you if your boss would let me get off the bus there one day after school. Maybe he'd even give me a job. I'm telling you, Mom, we need a computer at home. Everybody has one.

Anyway, I'm off to bed. Wake me up when you get home so I know you made it. Don't wake me up too much though. I got a big test in math tomorrow. Night!

Mark

I Am the Future

America has entered the Information Age. Adults realize that their children learn more about technology in their few years in school than they themselves ever will. Adults know that children have to be ready for a future much more complicated than today. So, they cater to children to give them as many advantages as possible. They also treat children as mini-adults because children seem to take today's changing world in stride better than they themselves. Study the scenarios below and indicate whether they are examples of adults catering to children or adults treating children as mini-adults.

	Cater	Mini-adult
1. Julie's four-year-old daughter is enrolled in ballet, soccer, and gymnastics.	_____	_____
2. The local TV station creates an all-kid format: kid shows, kid movies, kid commercials, and cartoons.	_____	_____
3. Nine-year-old Sam stays home alone for two hours after school every weekday.	_____	_____
4. Mrs. Mack buys three new books on how to raise healthy, intelligent, environmentally aware, emotionally stable kids.	_____	_____
5. Jeff buys his five-year-old son the Mega-power truck he just had to have after seeing it advertised on TV.	_____	_____
6. Ms. Sands asks her 13-year-old daughter if she thinks she should go out with a man from work.	_____	_____

Prefigurative Cultures

Margaret Mead, an anthropologist, defined America as a *prefigurative culture* which means things change so quickly in our world that children teach parents more than parents teach children. Do you think we live in a prefigurative culture? Indicate below which of the following things necessary for success as an adult you know more about than your parents, and which they know more about than you do.

	Parents Know More	I Know More
1. How to balance a checkbook	_____	_____
2. How to use the spellcheck on a computer program	_____	_____
3. How to figure tax on an item	_____	_____
4. How to figure the sale price of a discounted item	_____	_____
5. How to program the VCR	_____	_____
6. How to use a word processing program	_____	_____
7. How to use a graphics program	_____	_____
8. How to hook a VCR or computer game to a television set	_____	_____
9. How to make dinner	_____	_____
10. How to wash clothes	_____	_____
11. How to surf the Internet	_____	_____
12. How to act at a business meeting	_____	_____
13. How to give a speech	_____	_____
14. How to eat a balanced diet	_____	_____
15. How to raise children	_____	_____

Answers from Anthropology

Margaret Mead, an anthropologist, noticed three types of cultures around the world. Read the definitions of each type below and then give an example from your life or the life of a peer that exemplifies each type. Finally, indicate what type of a culture you think America will be when you are an adult.

Postfigurative Cultures: Children learn from their elders and ancestors. Individuals follow past traditions and change happens very slowly.

Example: _____

_____

_____

Configurative Cultures: Children learn from their peers. This happens often when a family emigrates to a very different culture and the children find that what they learn from other children is more useful in the new land than are the traditions from the old land.

Example: _____

_____

_____

Prefigurative Cultures: Children teach their parents. The world in a prefigurative culture changes so quickly that the beliefs and skills of adults are outdated and children are learning the skills needed for the future.

Example: _____

_____

_____

America's Future: Will the America of the future fit one of these culture types or be some combination of two or more of them? Describe what type of a culture America will be when you are an adult.

_____

_____

_____

Background

Perhaps five million human beings lived on this planet during the late Stone Age. Even when cities were being built and writing invented, when warriors rode in chariots and pyramids were rising, the world population was barely triple that. By the time of the Roman Empire, only one hundred generations ago, the world population was well under two hundred million—far fewer than live in the United States today.

In the last three centuries the numbers have exploded. In 1825 the world population was barely a billion. Today it approaches six billion. Even optimistic experts think it will reach the ten billion mark before it levels off, and that enormous total will likely be reached during the lifetime of today's children (2075).

With the advent of modern farming (high-yield seeds, inorganic fertilizers, mechanized planting and harvesting, and powerful pesticides) and the intensive application of scientific methods, we could adequately meet the nutritional needs of ten billion people (but not at the same living standard to which Westerners are accustomed). However, shortages of water, energy, clean air, minerals, and trees will be problems long before the ten billion mark is reached. In fact, given the shrinkage of natural resources and the pollution and interference with the ecosystem that today's six billion people cause, it can be argued that planet earth is extremely overpopulated today. The only question is what force—starvation, disease, war, or population control—will bring our numbers down to a level that can be sustained.

In this lesson, students struggle with the issues that overpopulation produces and contemplate ways to nurture the planet that will allow it to maintain human habitation.

Understanding the Reading

Following a reading of the senator's plea for foreign aid monies to be used to raise the level of education and standard of living in foreign lands, students should be able to answer the following questions:

1. Why does the senator believe feeding the hungry is not a worthy cause in and of itself? (because the world has a larger problem of overpopulation and an ample food supply encourages population growth)

2. What does the senator believe would be a more worthy way to spend foreign aid money? (on the modernization of other nations because higher education levels and standards of living lead to zero population growth)

3. What factors seem to discourage high birth rate? (education, social and political freedoms, the availability of productive work, and a decent standard of living)

4. What does the senator believe foreign aid monies should be spent on? (factories, libraries, democracy, and education for the peoples of other lands)

Teaching Activities

1. What constitutes an ideal birth rate and population density? Allow students to consider various aspects of the debate on population growth by assigning the "Baby Boom" activity.

2. Many advancements in agriculture have transformed the hunting and gathering societies of the past into the large-scale farming world of today. Allow students to trace the steps of the advancements by assigning research into the dates and significance of various farming techniques with "A Farming Time Line" activity.

Extensions

1. Assign the completion of an opinion essay in which students describe what they believe to be the ideal conditions of living, including climate and population density.

2. Assign research into China's population control laws. What are the pros and cons of such strict regulations?

3. Require students to research areas where overcrowding leads to many families living together, such as Japan, and areas where the sparse population requires families to travel many miles just to see a doctor or buy food.

My Fellow Senators,

Each year America spends billions of dollars on foreign aid feeding and clothing the peoples of other lands, while here at home we step over our own homeless when we walk down the streets and fund soup kitchens to feed our own population of hungry citizens. If feeding the rest of the world were a wise practice, I would be an avid supporter. But let's consider the facts.

Hunger is the result of relative overpopulation: too little food, too many to feed. Historically, overpopulation has always been a problem. It has even been suggested that the transformation of society from hunting and gathering tribes to agricultural communities was a result of population pressures. Because farming could produce food more effectively and support a denser population, human population continued to grow following the transformation. In fact—here's the important point— population tends to grow to whatever level the food supply will support, and then some.

So when we feed the peoples of the world, we cause more problems than we correct. Today's generation may get fed, but tomorrow's generation gets larger. An ample food supply encourages growth. Modernization, on the other hand, tends to reduce population growth to a zero level—one or two children per woman. Education, social and political freedoms, the availability of productive work, and a decent standard of living all seem to discourage high birth rates.

If we insist on spending billions of dollars in foreign aid, we need to reconsider what that money is spent on. Raising the level of education and the standard of living in foreign lands is what will slow population growth while food distribution will speed it up. Overpopulation is a cancer that affects the entire world and threatens its future existence. Feeding today's generation of hungry is like putting a Band-Aid on a cancerous sore without addressing the cancer itself. Whether it is Somalia or Bangladesh, let's give them factories and libraries and democracy, not the proverbial free lunch.

Baby Boom

What constitutes an ideal birth rate and population density is—and has long been—debated. Consider the following aspects and decide for yourself what a sensibly sized population looks like. Answer the questions on a separate sheet of paper.

1. Historically, governments believed that population growth meant an increase in national power and importance. Today the thinking has been reversed and most countries discourage high birth rates. What arguments exist in favor of each way of thinking? Why was the previous attitude sensible then and the current one sensible now?

2. Why would high birth rates (lots of babies per family) be advantageous in a society that is primarily agricultural? Why would high birth rates be disadvantageous in an even earlier society that hunts and gathers? Why would high birth rates be disadvantageous in a modern, industrial society?

3. It is sometimes argued that the entire world population could fit into the state of Alaska, and that the earth is, therefore, not overpopulated. Is this a reasonable argument? Why or why not?

4. Human beings are remarkably adaptable to any climate. Population expansion began earliest in semi-arid temperate river valleys. Today there are cities in every possible climate. Why is this possible? (Consider especially food and energy distribution systems.)

5. What would you consider to be an ideal population for a community? For a nation? For the world?

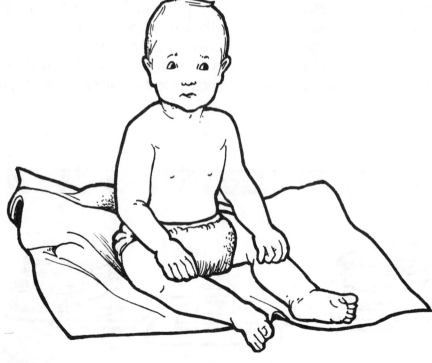

A Farming Time Line

Before true agriculture (the clearing of the natural habitat to plant crops), there was harvesting of wild grasses, roots, and berries. Research the following sequential list of advancements that have transformed the hunting and gathering society of the past into the large-scale farming society of today. Find the approximate date of each advancement and other information available on its significance to agriculture.

	DATE OF INVENTION	SIGNIFICANCE TO AGRICULTURE
Pointed sticks for planting	_____	_____
Stone axes for felling trees	_____	_____
Stone-edged scythes	_____	_____
Use of draft animals	_____	_____
Dung fertilizers	_____	_____
Chemical fertilizers	_____	_____
Iron and steel plows	_____	_____
Mechanical equipment	_____	_____
Improvement of seed stock	_____	_____
Irrigation methods	_____	_____
Pesticides	_____	_____

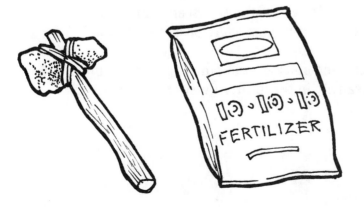

Today's Toys Tomorrow's Talents

Background

Although formal education has long played an important role in preparing children for adulthood, there is no telling how many life skills are refined through strategic games of chess, inventive play with blocks, and make-believe tea parties attended by dolls and teddy bears.

Some toys and games have changed very little over the years. In the absence of any hype or advertising, the Slinky—invented by an engineer in 1945 and named by his wife for the strange movements it makes—was purchased by 2.5 million consumers in 1995. Yet most toys have undergone some updating. The latest Barbie item is a computer software package that allows its user to design, model on the screen, print out, and piece together actual dresses to be worn by the doll. Monopoly players can now play the game with opponents from around the world via the Internet being assured that the currency conversions will be taken care of by the computer with each international move. Whereas boys of yesteryear played with metal soldiers, today's boys push buttons and move joysticks to destroy human enemies and battleships from space.

In this lesson, students examine the direction of play, make judgments about the value and effectiveness of toys used to entertain as well as to educate, and predict the future of children's free-time interests.

Understanding the Reading

Following a reading of the grandmother's letter to a toy company, students should be able to answer the following questions:

1. Why does the grandparent believe that such novelty toys as Slime, Gak, Foam, and Kooshballs sell? (because of the high-intensity advertising on TV channels programmed entirely for children)

2. What are the advantages and disadvantages of playing video games? (Advantages—develops fine motor skills, quick decision-making skills, and quick reflex reactions. Disadvantages—decreases attention span, allows for little imagination or creativity, the content is often aggressive or even violent.)

3. Will the skills of quick reflexes and quick decision making be more important than those of imagination and creativity in the future? (Answers will vary.)

Teaching Activities

1. It has been suggested that play is a child's work. Require students to evaluate toys of today and of past years on the educational value of each with the use of "The Importance of Play" activity.

2. How do toys today differ from those of the past? Do boys and girls play with different toys? Is there more value in playing with pots and pans or store-bought toys? Divide students into groups of three or four so they can address such questions together with the use of the "Critically Considering Creativity" activity.

3. Allow students to create their own toy with "The Ultimate Toy" activity. You may wish to require students to create a prototype of the toy they write about and draw.

Extension

1. Ask students to research the invention of a single toy or game, or allow them to research the toys and games of various countries and/or time periods.

2. Have students create a prototype of the toy they wrote about and drew in "The Ultimate Toy" activity.

3. Ask students to imagine they are representatives from the Santa's Elves Toy company. They are to write a response to the concerned grandparent whose letter they have read. They should address the concerns of the grandparent, perhaps explaining that tin is no longer used because it is not safe or that many of the toys in Santa's Elves' line are fun and educational. They may even offer the grandparent a coupon or gift certificate for a specific item that the grandparent may enjoy.

Dear Santa's Elves Toy Company,

I urge you to consider making old-fashioned toys in the old-fashioned way once again. The toys coming out of your factory today do not deserve to bear the name of Santa's elves! Santa's real elves make wooden blocks and bouncing balls, sticks of clay and jars of paint, tin soldiers and dolls that cry and blink their eyes. A child can build a whole city with wooden blocks. A child can learn to parent with a doll that cries. A child can mold clay into creative shapes and become a little artist. A child can invent a myriad of games with bouncing balls. What is a child to do with a glob of sticky, gluey green stuff that holds no shape or a stringy ball that looks as though it is made of cut up rubber bands and can neither bounce nor roll? The only reason such "toys" even sell is that huge advertising companies bombard young ones with cute and clever commercials that run over and over again on the all-children-shows networks on television.

Of course children are watching the television programs, or playing some video game on the television set, because they have no real toys to play with. The video games probably teach quick decision-making and improve fine motor skills and reaction time, but there is little creativity in blowing up enemy space ships with the flick of a joystick. Furthermore, such fast-paced visually explicit video worlds decrease a child's attention span and world of imagination even more than television shows themselves.

Yet if by some miracle a child discovers the world of real toys and games, that child is doomed to buy models inferior to the ones I played with in my day. Your company puts out a jacks game complete with plastic jacks. Tin soldiers have been replaced with plastic soldiers. Paper dolls are now made with paper so thin that the entire activity becomes unusable after a single afternoon game. Adult life is hard enough in today's world; please do not take away the joys of childhood.

Sincerely,
A concerned grandparent

The Importance of Play

Play is important to the development of a child for it is through play that a child learns many of the skills and rules he or she will use in adult life. List below seven toys that children played with when your parents were children and seven toys that children play with today. Then look at the Value Box below and list all of the values that apply to each of the toys you have listed. According to the listed values, do toys of today or of yesteryear offer children more?

VALUE BOX

Encourages creativity	Includes academic knowledge	Teaches math skills
Develops fine motor skills	Develops artistic talents	Encourages imagination
Teaches social skills	Is entertaining, fun	Includes decision-making
Teaches how to follow rules	Teaches taking turns	Develops strategy skills

---

Toys Played with in My Parents' Day   **Value of Toy**

1. _____   _____
2. _____   _____
3. _____   _____
4. _____   _____
5. _____   _____
6. _____   _____
7. _____   _____

Toys Played with in My Day   **Value of Toy**

1. _____   _____
2. _____   _____
3. _____   _____
4. _____   _____
5. _____   _____
6. _____   _____
7. _____   _____

Critically Considering Creativity

Discuss with your group the following questions and assign a recorder to write your group's answers on a separate sheet of paper. Be prepared to share your answers with the class.

1. Do you think there is more value in playing with store-bought toys or boxes, pots, pans, and other odds and ends found around the house? Which did you spend more time playing with as a young child?

2. How do toys today differ from the toys your parents played with? Do today's toys develop the skills tomorrow's adults will need?

3. Do boys and girls play with different types of toys? If so, which types do each play with?

4. What skills are learned and what talents are reinforced through play with technological toys? Are these important skills and talents for future adults to have?

5. How do you think toys will be different in 30 years?

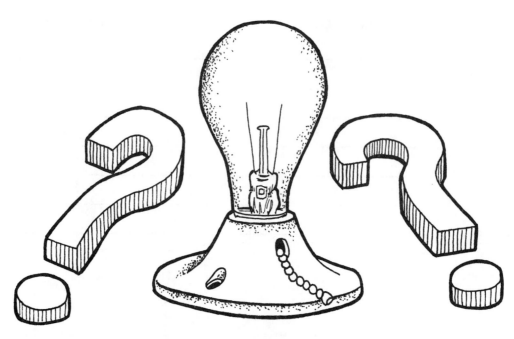

The Ultimate Toy

Develop the ultimate toy. It must be exciting, entertaining, educational, and pleasing to boys, girls, and parents. The toy may assume the use of any materials and/or technology available in today's world. Write a detailed description on a separate sheet of paper of how the toy works and draw a picture of the toy below. You may even wish to create a prototype out of boxes, cardboard, and other household materials to share with your classmates.

Endangered Species

Background

Worldwide it is estimated that more than a thousand species of animals become extinct every year. A thousand species of birds and 700 species of animals including the mountain gorilla, jaguar, leopard, cheetah, rhinoceros, African elephant, and 23 types of whales are on the verge of vanishing.

Exploration, colonization, and population expansion have been responsible for much of this mass extinction. Humans have introduced predator species into areas where they have wiped out the native species of animals, destroyed the natural habitats of wetland and forest dwellers, and created pollution that kills birds, fish, and reptiles. But the greatest culprit in silencing our forests and lakes is that of indiscriminate hunting and fishing. In a single year in the nineteenth century, a single foreign port unloaded from the Americas 127,000 beaver pelts, 30,000 marten, 110,000 raccoon, and 16,000 bear. Similar horror stories can be told about the bison, passenger pigeon, seal, otter, fox, and walrus. In a continent once teeming with wild animals, it is now unusual to see a fox, beaver, or wolf.

In this lesson, students study possible causes of animal extinction and make personal judgments about hunting, fishing, polluting, and conducting research with animals.

Understanding the Reading

Following a reading of the Letter to the Editor, students should be able to answer the following questions:

1. What are some of the causes of animal extinction? (destruction of the habitat of various animals, various types of pollution, the introduction of predators into new areas, and indiscriminate hunting and fishing)

2. Which cause does the author of the letter consider the most destructive? (hunting and fishing)

3. What are some of the reasons man has hunted for animals throughout history? (for sport, food, fur, or animal parts such as tusks, skins, oils, bones, and feathers)

4. In what way does the author of this letter suggest that the extermination of animals today differs from the extinction of dinosaurs 65 million years ago? (The dinosaurs became extinct due to some natural disaster while the mass extinction of animals today is a consciously conducted catastrophe.)

Teacher Activities

1. It can be debated that animal research is another example of humankind's ill-treatment of animals. The debate on animal research covers a wide range of views from those who oppose any type of animal research to those who accept the use of animals in the research of the causes and cures of diseases but not the research used to create safe cosmetics, to those who accept the use of animals for research when animals are not made to suffer unnecessarily, to those who do not oppose any kind of animal research. Allow students to discover and voice their own opinions on the issue by assigning the "Animal Research" activity.

2. What is the endangered species IQ of each student in the class? Allow students to test their knowledge and learn interesting facts about animals who are on the verge of extinction with the "Animals in Danger" activity.

Extension

1. Study various endangered species in depth. What does it mean for an animal to be endangered? How does it get the title "endangered"? Assign a research project on the lifestyle, habitat, eating habits, etc. of an endangered animal. Be certain students include in their reports just why the animal has become endangered.

2. Explore the domestication of the dog, cat, cow, pig, and chicken, and discuss the evolutionary changes that domestication entails.

3. Poll students on what unusual wild animals they have seen during their lifetimes outside of zoo walls. Do not count raccoon, deer, mice, rats, skunks, or squirrels. Then ask students to consider what animals the pioneers might have run into when they first arrived in this country.

Key for "Animals in Danger"

1. The timberwolf was considered dangerous to humans and was hated by ranchers who believed it killed their livestock.

2. In determining what animals are likely to become extinct, consider the number of offspring per year, the ability to flee or fight, intelligence, adaptability, and the previous absence of predators.

3. 127,000 beaver pelts, 30,000 marten, 110,000 raccoon, and 16,000 bear

4. 1,000 species of birds, 23 types of whales, and 700 other animal species

Dear Editor,

In your January 6 edition of *People for the Planet,* you ran an article which suggested that the one thousand or more species which become extinct every year are meeting their doom due to pesticides, oil spills, toxic wastes, and the human population expansion. These factors not only destroy the natural habitat of wetland and forest dwelling animals, but also introduce new predators to areas where they wipe out existing species. Although these are causes, you have missed the single largest reason for the silence in our forests and lakes—indiscriminate hunting and fishing.

Hunting, whether for sport, food, fur, or animal parts, has played havoc with wildlife for thousands of years. The ancient Egyptians killed off all the elephants and giraffes near the Nile, the ancient Greeks their lions and leopards, and the ancient Romans all the hippos, rhinoceroses, and zebras of North Africa.

In the last 500 years, hunting has reached cataclysmic proportions. In America 5 billion passenger pigeons were entirely massacred along with nearly all of the land's 60 million bison. Beaver, marten, wolf, bear, seal, otter, and fox were trapped or shot in numbers that are almost inconceivable. In the nineteenth century, the seal trade took perhaps 60 million skins and the walrus trade an estimated 4 million. Oceans once so thick with fish that one merely rowed out from shore a dozen yards and brought them up with a bucket are now almost barren. Skies once filled with bluebirds, cardinals, flickers, and scarlet tanagers are now quiet.

The estimated thousand-plus species that become extinct every year are not victims of neglect or short-sightedness. They are victims of willful and deliberate hunting and fishing. This degree of extermination is on the order of the natural cataclysm that made the dinosaurs extinct 65 million years ago. The difference is this mass extinction has been consciously committed.

An ex-hunter

Animal Research

Although scientists never use animals on the endangered list, animal research is another example of humankind's ill-treatment of animals. Discuss the following questions with the members of your group and elect a secretary to record your responses on a separate sheet of paper so that you will be prepared to share your thoughts with the entire class.

1. Do you believe researchers should be allowed to use animals to conduct experiments? If so, what factors should be considered in deciding when research on animals is warranted?

2. Do you believe medical and biological science would see the same advancements as it does now if animal research were banned altogether? What are some alternative research methods that could be used to discover cures to diseases or workings of the human mind and body?

3. Do human beings have the responsibility to protect animals? If so, where should we draw the line? Is eating meat okay? Wearing furs? Destroying an animal's natural habitat? Hunting? Fishing? Animal research for the purpose of providing consumers with safe cosmetics? Animal research for the sake of disease prevention and cures?

Animals in Danger

What's your endangered species IQ? See if you can answer the questions below. Consult your teacher for the answers. Research each topic further for more information.

1. The timber wolf was hunted almost to extinction in America from a wide-ranging population of millions. Yet it is not good for meat or for fur and has no useful parts. Why was it hunted?

2. What made the dodo bird and the passenger pigeon so susceptible to extinction while others like the deer, raccoon, and skunk survived so well?

3. In a single year in the nineteenth century, one French port unloaded from the Americas beaver, marten, raccoon, and bear furs. Guess how many of each were unloaded in one year.

4. How many species of birds, whales, and other animals are now on the verge of extinction?

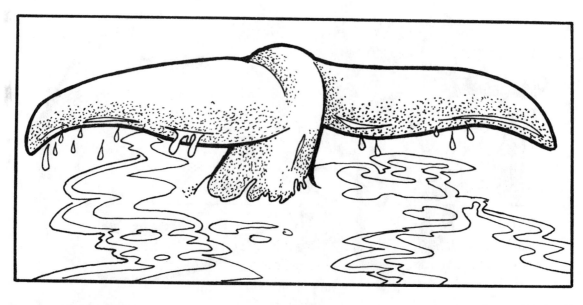

Background

Computer graphics programs can create your company's ads, design your wedding invitations, or draw banners for your daughter's tenth birthday party. A synthesizer can write, print out, and play music of its own creation. Computers working with x-rays and sonograms can show a person what part of the brain is active during logical thought processing or just what the baby inside a woman's uterus looks like.

It seems technology is creating for us. Doctors now spend less time wondering, contemplating, and creating theories about the workings of the body and brain and more time making the public aware of what computers have discovered, suggested, or proved. Artists spend less time composing music and painting pictures and more time editing computer-generated sounds and images.

Has the beginning of the Information Age spelled the end of human creativity? Retro-music and movies based on books from the nineteenth century and TV shows from the fifties seem to suggest so. The absence of philosophy classes at the college level seems to suggest so. Cut-backs in music and the arts in elementary schools seem to suggest so. Have we created technology that now creates for us?

In this lesson, students contemplate the meaning of creativity and consider what it might mean in the future.

Understanding the Reading

Following a reading of the opening remarks of Ms. Simmons and Mr. Dickens, speaking on a radio show program focusing on creativity, students should be able to answer the following questions.

1. How would Ms. Simmons define *creativity*? (She would say it involves the bringing into being of something completely new.)

2. How would Mr. Dickens define creativity? (He believes the new creativity to involve organizing and utilizing the vast amount of information available today.)

3. In what ways does Ms. Simmons suggest the ordinary person has lost his/her creativity? (The individual person no longer needs to write letters, answer questions, invent workable solutions to problems, or draw pictures in the advent of technology.)

4. What do you suppose Mr. Dickens meant by, "Creative people are willing to think of creative new definitions for creativity"? (He meant that Ms. Simmons was being too narrow and uncreative herself in her definition of creativity.)

Teaching Activities

1. Is creativity important in our age of information? Is it important that everyone exercise creativity or just that artists do? Do we see creativity only in museums or in the common everyday workplace as well? Require students to formulate and express their own opinions on the place of creativity in today's society by assigning them the questions in the "Creatively Defining Creativity" activity. Students should be divided into groups of three or four to encourage discussion of the questions. Each group may wish to designate a recorder to record responses so that each group can share its ideas with the entire class.

2. Allow students to use their own creativity to design and construct a building. Students may choose to construct a hotel, a home, an office building, a school, etc. As a first step, assign the "Building a Building" activity which directs students to draw the floor plans for their buildings and to decide on their interior designs. Then have students construct their buildings with blocks, cardboard boxes, wallpaper, and carpet scraps, etc.

Extension

1. Assign research of the scientific definition of creativity. What do educators consider creativity to mean? How do artists define creativity? Have psychologists and brain physiologists discovered creative parts of the brain or brain chemicals responsible for creativity? Does it seem to be an inherited talent? Can one "learn" creativity?

2. Allow students to work in groups to compose and present a song, or draw and display a mural.

3. Assign research, individually or in groups, of various creative people from artists to dancers to photographers to authors to performers.

4. Allow your class to create its own play or performing arts show. Students may choose to base their performance on a story they have read in language arts, or they may create a new story.

Technology versus Creativity

Tonight we welcome Mr. Dickens, a professor of computer research skills at IMU, and Ms. Simmons, the head of the English Literature Department at LMI. Ms. Simmons argues that human creativity has been replaced by technology in our modern world. Mr. Dickens suggests that creativity is not dead but that the face of it has changed. Let's hear their opening remarks. Ms. Simmons.

Ms. Simmons: Thank you, Lynn. There continue to be, of course, creative geniuses in the modern world. They program computers, write catchy advertisements, and create the ever-shrinking examples of art we find in museums and in well-written books. However, the everyday person is not as creative as he or she once was. No one knows how to write an eloquent letter anymore because the use of the telephone or a quick E-mail message is an easier way to communicate. No one has to look around the house for something that will make a window stop rattling or a picture hang straight. We go to the store and buy just the thing that someone else has designed and mass marketed just for the purpose. Computers research answers for us, draw pictures for us, and produce massive amounts of material goods to handle any problem that ever arises. We no longer need to think, imagine, or create. And, on the whole, we don't.

Mr. Dickens: Ms. Simmons is holding onto the old image of creativity wherein individuals write books, paint pictures, compose music, and concoct new inventions. We don't need many of these people anymore. We have entered the Information Age. The computers know how to write music and draw pictures. They hold enough information to answer any question you can ask and devise a solution to the greatest of problems. We don't need inventors; we need organizers. The new creativity stresses the ability to group, correlate, and utilize the vast information that is already out there. Creative people put old sounds together in new ways to create music with their computers. Creative people look at computer printouts on what areas of the brain are active during what types of activities and imagine what that knowledge can mean to medicine. Creative people put together graphics in new ways. Creative people are willing to think of creative new definitions for *creativity*.

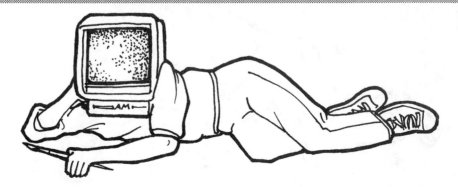

Creatively Defining Creativity

Discuss and answer the following questions with the other members of your group.

1. How would an artist define *creativity*? How would a scientist? How would you?

2. If necessity is the mother of invention, then are we reducing our need (and ability) to be inventive by creating computers that can do more and more things for us? Are we creating machines that will do our creating for us? Would this be a good or bad thing?

3. Is creativity important in the workplace or just in museums and in the music industry?

4. Where do you see the most creativity in today's world? In what fields do most creative people work today?

5. Medical researchers now use technology to design new drugs. Is this an example of computers doing the creating for us, or of people making creative use of technology?

6. How has creativity changed throughout history? (For example, consider that people before the inventions of the TV and radio had to create their own stories and entertain themselves, but people of the distant past could not be as creative in how they prepared food or dressed because the food and fabric choices were very limited.)

Building a Building

A great deal of creativity goes into the exterior and interior structures that we live, work, play, and shop in each day. Design and construct a building of your own. You may choose to create a house, office, school, store, or other building. Draw the floor plans below. Write ideas for the interior walls, floors, furniture, and wall hangings on a separate sheet of paper. Then use blocks, cardboard boxes, wallpaper, carpet scraps, and other art and household supplies to construct your building.

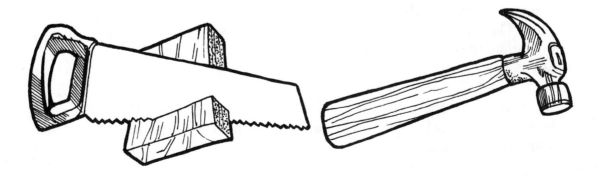

Man and Machines

Background

A machine is a device that performs a job and saves us physical labor. A combination of the three principles of the lever, the inclined plane, and the pulley have been used in the creation of primitive machines since earliest civilization. It was not until the invention of the steam engine, however, that the Industrial Revolution really got underway. Textile mills, steam locomotives, paddlewheel ships, and steel mills transformed the agricultural societies of England, America, and Germany into industrial societies. Machines were built for transportation, waging wars, farming, making consumer goods, and creating machine parts for more machines. The landscape was dotted with factories, mines, and railroad tracks; the cities were filled with smoke, fumes, and noise.

By the early twentieth century other countries had joined the race to industrialization, and today with the era of the electronic machines, America and a few other countries are in a Post-Industrial Age. This does not mean an end to machines, but instead machines are so advanced that they practically think for themselves. Robotics have replaced human beings on factory assembly lines. Computer chips are embedded in virtually all machines including children's toys. It is no longer a fantasy to imagine that the ultimate machines will not be that much different from those who make them.

In this lesson, students think about the future of technology and its meaning to tomorrow's world.

Understanding the Reading

Following a reading for the advertisement for Acres Green, students should be able to answer the following questions:

1. According to the advertisement, why did the United States take the lead in the Industrial Revolution? (availability of natural resources, size of country, social and political freedoms, absence of war on domestic soil)

2. What negative impacts of industrialization in nineteenth-century America were pointed out by the author of this article? (Factories were noisy and smoky, employees worked long hours in unventilated buildings, cities were overcrowded and had poor sanitation, tuberculosis and typhus ran rampant, and machines began to run the lives of people.)

3. What does the author of this ad fear is the future of technology? (Machines will become so advanced that they may take over the lives of human beings—do their jobs, make their decisions, etc.)

4. Would you like to live in a community like Acres Green? Why or why not? What would be the difficulties and drawbacks of establishing and maintaining such a community? (Answers will vary. Students should realize that medical, scientific, and technological advancements that make life longer and easier would be rejected in Acres Green. They should also acknowledge that any one area has a limited amount of natural resources and that a community that sections itself off from the rest of the world will have shortages.)

5. Although there continue to be some primitive tribes and lands throughout the world, most regions and peoples have opted to accept and make use of the world's increasingly more complicated machines. Why? Is it human nature that each generation should progress and invent more advanced machines, or is it smarter to live the simpler life of primitive peoples? (Answers will vary.)

Teaching Activities

1. In today's world we interact with so many machines in the course of our everyday lives that we take many of them for granted and hardly notice they are there. Require students to notice all the machines they use in a day by listing them in the "Machines in the Morning, Machines at Noontime, Machines at Suppertime" activity.

2. What is the future of machines? Will artificial intelligence replace employees in the workplace? Will medical technology advance to the point that tiny robots will one day scrub our arteries clean and repair tissues in our bodies? Allow students to think about the future of technology by assigning the questions from the "Machines of the Future" activity.

Extension

1. Explore the meaning and functions of the lever, the pulley, and the inclined plane. As a homework assignment, ask students to make a simple machine that performs a simple task. Students may wish to use rubber bands, small motors, Popsicle sticks, glue, batteries, utensils, coins, cardboard boxes, etc.

2. Watch the Charlie Chaplin movie *Modern Times,* which is about the Industrial Revolution.

3. Study the influence of warfare on the development of machines including the catapult, the submarine, the satellite, and advances in metallurgy for cannons, swords, and guns.

4. Divide students into groups of three or four and assign the invention of a new machine. Students should tell of the function and the workings of their inventions.

ACRES GREEN—ESCAPE THE RAT RACE

With the invention of the steam engine, England gave birth to the Industrial Revolution. Because of America's size and abundant natural resources, its relative isolation from wars, and its climate of political and social freedom, it quickly took the lead in building smoke-belching factories. America also took the lead in establishing overcrowded cities with poor sanitation teeming with tuberculosis and typhus, and long work hours of drudgery for workers in unventilated factories. A society where machines ran people instead of the other way around was created.

Technology marches on. Robots replace factory workers. Computer chips replace white collar workers. The cities are blighted war zones where new diseases replace the ones that have been conquered.

You can ride the band wagon and sing the praises of technology. You can marvel at the magical machines that save time, money, and lives. One day you may even marvel at a machine that feeds your children . . . makes your decisions . . . replaces your job . . . and takes over your life!

Or—you can escape the rat race. Acres Green is a self-supporting community of 253 people. We raise our own food and sew our own clothes without the use of tractors or sewing machines. We work the land with our hands and produce only what we need for the community of Acres Green. Presently we have the need for 1 carpenter and 20 farmhands. Join us for the harvest months or write for our information packet on creating a self-supporting community in your region.

ACRES GREEN—MACHINES NOT PERMITTED, HUMAN BEINGS REQUIRED!

Machines in the Morning, Machines at Noontime, Machines at Suppertime

We use so many machines in today's world that we take them for granted. Imagine the difference in your day if there were no ovens, blow dryers, cars, or toasters! List all of the machines you use in one day from the time you awake until the time you go to bed. Also consider and list the function or purpose of each machine used and how you would accomplish the purpose without the machine. How much longer would it take to accomplish simple functions without machines? Use the back of this page if necessary.

Machine Used	Function Accomplished	Time Needed With Machine	How to Do Without Machine	Time Needed Without Machine
1.				
2.				
3.				
4.				
5.				
6.				
7.				
8.				
9.				
10.				
11.				
12.				
13.				
14.				
15.				
16.				
17.				

Machines of the Future

With the era of the electronic machine, America has entered the Post-Industrial Age. This does not mean the end to machines, but rather machines so advanced they seem to reason for themselves. Think about the future of technology and answer the questions below on a separate sheet of paper.

1. Today, some robots are designed so small, they are invisible to the naked eye. Built by assembling individual atoms, such tiny robots might be used to scrub the inside of arteries or repair tissue, once someone comes up with batteries small enough to power them. What other uses could be made of such small robots if they were perfected?

2. Artificial intelligence refers to computers that will be able to "think" and make decisions in the same manner as human beings. Already we have computerized games that can think many moves ahead and that make decisions of their own based on incoming information. Do you believe computers will ever think entirely like human beings? In what ways might they never be the same as human beings? Might a computer fall in love? Refuse to work? Play tricks on its operator?

3. Will computers and electronics ever replace the entire work force? If so, what will human beings do with their time? How will they make their money? In 20 years will there be any jobs that do not require computer competence? Can you name any jobs today that require no knowledge of any simple or complex machine?

Background

In even the simplest and most primitive societies, there is some form of money. Without it, all transactions of goods and services would be done by barter or trade. Money simplifies the process. Yet as a medium of exchange, it has no intrinsic value. As long as the buyer and the seller agree to the stated value of money, it can be as plain as a piece of paper.

The American dollar is no longer what it used to be. Until the late 1960s it was fully backed by gold or silver coin. By international agreement, currencies around the world are now freefloating and backed by nothing but the promise of the country that prints the money.

Likely the next change will be that no paper or coin will be used at all. Increasingly money transactions have become computerized. The not-too-distant future may see all transactions accomplished by credit and debit cards. Whether such a system would be entirely stable is another question. Some economists foresee an eventual return to some kind of gold or silver standard. Others look to a global economy. Still others see cyberspace as the future of finance.

In this lesson, students read an argument in favor of a return to the gold standard and make a personal judgment about the future of finance. Students also create a Money

Understanding the Reading

Museum, study inflation and deflation, and examine the pros and cons of a barter system. Following a reading of the newspaper article in favor of returning to a gold standard, students should be able to answer the following questions:

1. What is the primary purpose of money? (It is used as a medium of exchange to simplify the barter process.)

2. How does money simplify the barter process? (It eliminates the need to exchange equal values of goods and services. A seller can collect money for the goods he sells and use it to buy what he wants or save it for another time.)

3. Why does Al Hurston argue in favor of a return to the gold standard? (He says saving money is risky and the accumulation of debt tempting, when money is not backed by gold.)

4. What do you think is the future of money in the United States? In the world? (Answers will vary. Possible answers include we will end up with a global economy, we will return to the gold standard, or all transactions will be done with credit cards and/or computers.)

Teaching Activities

1. Encourage students to consider how different cultures have come up with different items to use as currency by assigning the "Interesting Items of Exchange" activity. Students imagine there is suddenly no such thing as money, and it is up to them to determine what the country will use for currency now. The activity sheet lists seven possibilities, but students may think of some of their own. The activity sheet also lists criteria for deciding what will make good currency (easy to handle, fairly plentiful, resistant to decay or damage), but students may also come up with other criteria that should also be considered. Encourage such expansion of the ideas listed in the exercise.

2. Require students to investigate the fluctuation of the value of money by tracing the price of various goods in the business page of a local newspaper for five days. "The Ups and Downs of Money" activity sheet provides students with a place to record their findings. Lead a class discussion on the reasons for inflation and deflation and the ways in which money fluctuations affect the consumer.

Extension

1. Create a Money Museum by requiring each student to bring an item for display that has functioned as money at some time or place (jewelry, gems, shells, beads, domestic and foreign coins, animal teeth, etc.)

2. Assign the completion of research on the value of money—inflation and deflation. Encourage students to think about what would happen if every worker in the United States demanded a raise overnight. What happened to the value of the dollar during the Great Depression? Why?

3. Gold and silver have been used as money throughout the world for as long as 10,000 years. Research why. (Reasons include both are relatively rare, highly malleable, resistant to corrosion, easy to extract from ore, and highly attractive in decoration such as art and jewelry.)

G-7 Favors Return to Gold Standard
By Veronica Anderberg

Financial Markets were rocked today with the rumor that representatives from the G-7 summit meeting will announce tomorrow their recommendation for a return to the gold standard. The G-7, which is comprised of representatives of the seven major industrialized nations, meets regularly to discuss international trade and finance. The rumor that the G-7 will strongly urge abandonment of the free-floating currency system now being used has prompted dramatic sell-offs in stock markets around the world. The price of gold and silver shot up to record levels. Both the New York and the American exchanges closed early in frenzied trading.

Without denying that the G-7 favors a return to the gold standard, a spokesman at the Federal Reserve assured the public that no such monetary policy change is planned.

Leading private economists have favored a return to the gold standard for years believing it would restore stability to global money markets. According to Al Hurston, who publishes the *American Investor Newsletter*, all industrialized countries have amassed large national debts with the free-floating system. "Money," says Hurston, "must be anchored in a real commodity." Throughout history people have not only used gold and silver coin, but also copper ingots, blocks of tea, beads, shells, whale teeth, and beetle legs.

Money simplifies the transaction of goods and services which would otherwise have to be done by barter or trade. With money, reliable values can be assigned to services and goods so that it is not necessary to trade items of equal value. With a commodity as currency, it is also possible for a seller to save his earnings. "When nothing backs the currency," says Hurston, "saving money is risky and the accumulation of debt too tempting."

Hurston believes a gold standard today is necessary and inevitable.

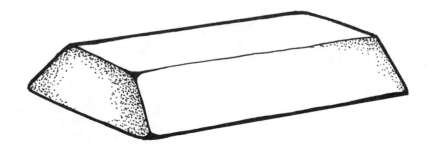

Interesting Items of Exchange

Imagine that suddenly there is no money, and it is up to you to find something to use as currency with which to buy and sell. Consider the usefulness of the following items as means of exchange. Do the items meet the currency criteria stated on the chart? Circle "yes" or "no" for each criterion when considering each item. Include a few of your own ideas for good items to use as currency in the spaces provided. Which would be the best item to use for currency? Why? In addition to the currency criteria listed below, what are some of the other pros and cons of using the items listed on this chart as currency?

Item	Currency Criterion		
	Easy to handle	Fairly plentiful	Resistant to decay or damage
Cans of soda	Yes No	Yes No	Yes No
Books	Yes No	Yes No	Yes No
Packs of gum	Yes No	Yes No	Yes No
Candy bars	Yes No	Yes No	Yes No
Colorful stones	Yes No	Yes No	Yes No
Videos	Yes No	Yes No	Yes No
Floppy disks	Yes No	Yes No	Yes No
_____ (Other)	Yes No	Yes No	Yes No
_____ (Other)	Yes No	Yes No	Yes No
_____ (Other)	Yes No	Yes No	Yes No

The Ups and Downs of Money

Money is a solid, tangible, real thing. You can see the shine of a nickel, hear the clink of quarters in a change purse, and feel the fold of a five dollar bill inside a birthday card. Yet the value of the money in your hand or in your wallet is not so real; it fluctuates from day to day. A loaf of bread that costs a dollar today may cost a dollar and ten cents next week.

Watch the fluctuation in the price of the various goods listed below by following the items in the business page of your local newspaper for five days in a row. How might the price changes you noted affect you at the grocery store or the gas station?

Barrel of oil		Ton of wheat		Ton of corn	
Date	Price	Date	Price	Date	Price
___	___	___	___	___	___
___	___	___	___	___	___
___	___	___	___	___	___
___	___	___	___	___	___
___	___	___	___	___	___

Ounce of silver		Ounce of gold	
Date	Price	Date	Price
___	___	___	___
___	___	___	___
___	___	___	___
___	___	___	___
___	___	___	___

Deadly Diseases

Background

Since the distant origins of humankind, we have struggled with the effects of viruses and bacteria. In the fourteenth and fifteenth centuries, the Bubonic Plague wiped out one third of Europe. Diseases brought from the Old World to the New World helped exterminate 80 percent of the indigenous people of America. Tuberculosis in the nineteenth century killed up to a quarter of Western civilization. Influenza in 1918-1919 took over 20 million lives worldwide. Throughout history, disease has killed far more people than war has.

Because infectious diseases require a certain concentration of people to sustain themselves, today's world is ripe for disease transmission. Few societies today remain isolated. Mega-cities have replaced small tribes, and modern transportation and global economies have turned many of us into world travelers. So, even with the antibiotics, vaccines, and improvements in sanitation, inspections, and insecticides that we have today, we still have been unable to conquer the spread of disease. Bacterial agents like tuberculosis and staphylococcus have developed immunity to many antibiotics, and other microbes have become highly resistant. AIDS has taken the lives of over 241,000 victims to date. Overcrowded cities, growing slums, unclean water supplies in many countries, and the increasingly mobile human population are helping spread new and mutant variants of old microbes faster than epidemiologists can track them.

In this lesson, students examine the terror of AIDS, cancer, and other life-threatening diseases and make their own judgments about how much money should be spent on the prevention, control, and cure of disease in the United States and throughout the world. After doing this, have students describe what the future of medicine might be like.

Understanding the Reading

Following a reading of the AIDS patient's letter to the president, students should be able to answer the following questions:

1. Why is the spread of disease so much easier in today's world than it was in ancient history? (Human populations are no longer small and isolated tribes.)

2. What two factors helped microbes spread during the Renaissance in Europe? (trade between Europe, Asia, Africa, and the Americas and the rapid growth of unsanitary cities)

3. Why did Mr. Skelly write this letter to the president? (He urged the president to budget more money to the research needed to control AIDS and other diseases.)

Teaching Activities

1. Medicine has a long and continuing history from the shamans of ancient times to modern surgical practices to organ transplants to genetic engineering. Require students to complete research on the various stages in medical history by completing the time line of the "An Apple a Day" activity. Any encyclopedia as well as various medical history books will assist students in learning about the history of medicine.

2. Occupational diseases are common in industrial societies. Four major types of occupational hazards face today's workers. *Biological hazards* refer to exposure to infectious diseases in humans, plants, and animals. *Physical hazards* include exposure to noise, heat, cold, and radiation. *Dust diseases* are contracted by miners and those exposed to other disease-causing dusts such as asbestos, cotton, and certain metals. *Chemical hazards* face those who manufacture or work with pesticides, plastics, industrial solvents, and other chemicals. Require students to examine occupational hazards by completing the "Work May Be Hazardous to Your Health" activity.

Extension

1. Allow students to write a persuasive essay or speech defending their position on the following question. Considering that disease has killed far more people than war throughout history, do you think the U.S. budget should contribute less money to defense and more money to the prevention and control of diseases? Why or why not?

2. Assign individual students or groups of students to research various diseases that do not kill but do affect a person's entire life. Assign the composition of a paper or performing of a speech that tells the reader or listener just what it means to be blind or deaf, or to live with another life-altering disease.

3. In nineteenth century England and America tuberculosis patients were required to live in sanitariums to protect others from infection. Should this be done with AIDS patients today? Ask students to defend a position. Require them to include information on why this is not the case in today's world.

4. Require students to create a time line of diseases that have haunted humanity throughout the ages. What medical advancements have eliminated various diseases of the past?

Dear Mr. President,

I am dying of AIDS. How I became infected is not important now. More than one million people in this country carry this terrible virus. They contracted it in many ways. In the next ten years, almost all of them will die of it.

Throughout history, viruses and bacteria have been killing human beings. However, deadly microbes historically had two disadvantages. The first is that human populations used to be fairly isolated, and they became resistant to the local diseases. Second, the human populations were small, and an infectious disease must have a certain concentration of people in order to thrive. Measles, for example, needs a minimum of a few hundred thousand. With most of humanity living in tribes, epidemic disease was less of a threat.

By the time of the Renaissance in Europe, microbes got past these two disadvantages. Trade between Europe, Asia, Africa, and the Americas allowed microbes to jump to areas where people had no resistance to them. And with the rapid growth of cities, microbes had the concentrations of people they needed to survive and to spread. Because sanitation in these growing cities was abominable, microbes also found easy routes of transmission—sewage and vermin.

The results of these factors were frightening. Plagues like the Bubonic killed one of every three Europeans in the fourteenth and fifteenth centuries. Diseases carried to the Americas helped exterminate eight out of every ten Native Americans. In the nineteenth century tuberculosis killed one of four in the Western world. The influenza pandemic of 1918-1919 killed one of every hundred people world-wide.

Antibiotics, vaccines, better sanitation, and pesticides have all helped to limit such epidemics in the modern world. But new diseases, like AIDS, need great attention. I urge you to fund more research in controlling them.

Sincerely,

J. L. Skelly

J.L. Skelly

An Apple a Day

Look into a book of medical history or in an encyclopedia under "Medicine" to find out what was happening in the world of medicine at the times listed below. Write a one- to two-sentence summary of the major trends below. What changes do you predict for the future of medicine?

Primitive Medicine   _____

                                          _____

                                          _____

Medieval Europe   _____

                                          _____

                                          _____

The Renaissance   _____

                                          _____

                                          _____

Seventeenth Century   _____

                                          _____

                                          _____

Eighteenth Century   _____

                                          _____

                                          _____

Nineteenth Century   _____

                                          _____

                                          _____

Twentieth Century   _____

                                          _____

                                          _____

Future Medicine   _____

                                          _____

                                          _____

Work May Be Hazardous to Your Health

In an industrialized society, there are risks of contracting various diseases from the chemicals, dusts, bacteria, etc. that you come into contact with on the job. Four major types of occupational hazards face today's workers. Think of what each of the following workers comes into contact with on the job, and check which types of hazard each worker may be in danger of. Discuss with classmates what specific physical, chemical, infectious, or dust hazards face each worker.

Worker	Type of Hazard			
	Infectious (plant, animal, or human)	Physical (noise, heat, cold, radiation)	Dust (metals and asbestos)	Chemical (pesticides and industrial solvents)
Farmer				
Hospital Worker				
Coal Miner				
Dry Cleaner				
Teacher				
Painter				
Jack Hammer Operator				
Scientist				

Background

Had it not been for the cleverness of human beings in harnessing energy, we would never have advanced beyond the early Stone Age, with muscular brawn still the only available force to accomplish work. The progress of civilization has depended on various sources of energy.

Draft animals (oxen, asses, and horses) for pulling carts and plows and for riding were the first advance in energy production—dating back as early as 4000 B.C.—after the use of fire. Fire, and the deliberate burning of wood, dates back half a million years. Windmills in Persia in 500 B.C. and waterwheels in Egypt in 300 B.C. were both used for irrigation purposes, and later for grinding grain. Yet historically, wood has been the most universally demanded fuel—used for cooking, heating, and smelting ore.

It was not until the seventeenth century that the burning of peat and coal supplanted wood as a fuel. Then in 1859, the first real oil well was drilled in Pennsylvania, and the petroleum industry began its rapid growth. Oil now furnishes 40 percent of the world's energy needs. Coal provides 28 percent, natural gas 20 percent, and nuclear power and renewable sources (geothermal, wind, solar, etc.) together provide the remaining 12 percent.

The Industrial Revolution depended on the use of fossil fuels which have helped transform us from an agrarian society into a post-industrial one. However, known resources of oil will be gone at current consumption rates in about 60 years. Coal could last hundreds of years but has serious drawbacks due to its pollutant effects. Technological advances in renewable sources of energy need to continue to bring the cost of wind turbine, solar, geothermal, and hydroelectric energy sources into price ranges where they can compete with fossil fuels if we are to continue to advance.

In this lesson, students examine the history of the harnessing of energy on our planet and make predictions about future energy sources.

Understanding the Reading

Following a reading of the alien's report to the Alpha Centauri Galactic Council, students should be able to answer the following questions:

1. What six advancements in energy did the alien suggest summarize the energy sources used on the planet Earth? (draft animals, windmills, waterwheels, peat and coal, petroleum, and nuclear fission)

2. What is meant by the term *renewable energy source*? (A renewable energy source is one that does not present us with a limited supply such as oil or coal. These sources include wind, water, solar, and geothermal energies.)

3. Why does the alien suggest that the use of coal and petroleum would not be a good idea even if the supplies were not limited? (The pollution from these energy sources damages the environment.)

4. Why did the use of peat and coal replace the use of wood in Europe 300 hundred years ago? (The timber supply was dwindling.)

Teaching Activities

1. Changes in the way energy is harnessed have marked new stages in human history. Explore with students the historical changes that can be attributed to various advancements in the harnessing of energy by assigning the "Energy and Historical Change" activity.

2. After students have attempted to match the breakthroughs in energy use with the historical results listed in the exercise, share with them the answers and background behind the answers as presented on the "Energy and Historical Change Answer Sheet."

Extensions

1. Assign either individuals or groups the diagramming, or even the creation, of a simple electrical device such as a buzzer, light, or bell.

2. Have each student bring to class a tool or toy that harnesses or holds energy. For example: pinwheel, rubber band-powered airplane, wind-up watch, whistling tea kettle, spring latch, slingshot, pencil sharpener, cap gun, sailboat.

3. Assign the research of a renewable source of energy. How is it harnessed? How expensive is it compared to fossil fuels? How effectively and to what extent is it used today? Is it likely to be a major energy source in the future with improved technology?

4. Assign further research into some of the breakthroughs in energy use and the historical results they listed in the "Energy and Historical Change" activity.

5. Use creative imagination in a class discussion—think of forms of energy that could be harnessed, no matter how absurd they are. Examples include raindrops, grass growing, ocean waves, lightning, and dogs scratching.

Official Report to the Alpha Centauri

Galactic Council

Inhabitants of Planet GG46 ("Earth"), who call themselves "human beings," have made amazing progress. Since our last visit 10,000 years ago, they have gone from using chipped stone tools to using electronic computing devices. As you requested, we have studied their development of energy sources. As you know, at the time of our last visit they were still burning sticks for the cooking of animal meats. A brief summary follows:

ENERGY SOURCE	LOCATION OF USE	PURPOSE	DATE
Draft Animals	Middle East	Pull carts, plows	6,000 yrs ago
Windmills	Persia	Irrigation	2,500 yrs ago
Waterwheels	Egypt	Irrigation	2,300 yrs ago
Peat and Coal	Europe	Replace timber	300 yrs ago
Petroleum	All over planet	Electricity, vehicles	100 yrs ago
Nuclear Fission	Industrial countries	Electricity	30 yrs ago

As the Council can see, advances in energy production are accelerating. Earth civilization, however, still depends on nonrenewable fossil fuels for 94 percent of its energy needs, and these are running out. Petroleum might last them another hundred years, coal a few hundred, but pollution from these sources seems to be damaging the environment already (as happened on AT22, now uninhabitable). Human beings are finding alternative renewable sources, especially wind, solar, and geothermal, but fusion is still beyond them and anti-gravity a fantasy.

PROGNOSIS: In a thousand years they will either be extinct or visiting us.

Energy and Historical Change

Test your energy IQ. See if you can match the breakthroughs in energy use listed in column A with the appropriate historical results in column B. Your teacher has the correct answers and can provide you with brief background on each correct response.

ENERGY BREAKTHROUGH

Nuclear fission

Oxen and mules

Oil refineries

Sailing ships

Steam engine

Electricity

Fired furnaces

Horses

Gunpowder cannons

Solid-fuel rockets

HISTORICAL RESULT

Space Age

Decline of feudalism

Age of Exploration

Interstate highway system

Industrial Revolution

Cold war

Development of agriculture

Bronze Age

Modern communications

Greek and Roman Empires

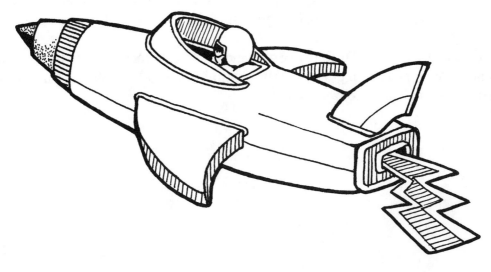

Energy and Historical Change Answer Sheet

NUCLEAR FISSION—COLD WAR: Einstein's formula $E = mc^2$ led to such frightening weapons that the superpowers have not risked all-out war for 50 years.

OXEN AND MULES—DEVELOPMENT OF AGRICULTURE: Using draft animals to draw plows dramatically increased tilled acreage and crop yields so that human beings could settle and build towns and cities.

OIL REFINERIES—INTERSTATE HIGHWAY SYSTEM: Refining crude oil into gasoline, diesel fuel, and jet engine fuel made possible the remarkable transportation system that is the foundation of today's global village.

SAILING SHIPS—AGE OF EXPLORATION: Highly sophisticated sails for wind power enabled the great explorers to visit the Americas, Africa, and the Far East.

STEAM ENGINE—INDUSTRIAL REVOLUTION: Burning coal to boil water into steam to drive pistons was a breakthrough that took people into the age of machines.

ELECTRICITY—MODERN COMMUNICATIONS: Controlling the flows of electricity made possible the telegraph, telephone, radio, television, and computers.

FIRED FURNACES—BRONZE AGE: When people of the Stone Age learned to melt ores and fashion copper and bronze tools, civilization took one of its greatest strides toward the modern age.

HORSES—GREEK AND ROMAN EMPIRES: Horses used for pulling supply wagons as well as for chariot and cavalry permitted the wars of conquest that built early empires.

GUNPOWDER CANNONS—DECLINE OF FEUDALISM: The fortified stone castles of Europe were not effective against cannons and other changes in warfare that brought an end to the medieval way of life and a beginning to centralized governments.

SOLID-FUEL ROCKETS—SPACE AGE: Solid and liquid fuel rockets were used in boosting manned and unmanned space probes for the Gemini and Apollo programs through which we have learned so much about our solar system.

Background

The history of psychoactive drugs dates to the very start of civilization. Primitive tribes of prehistory apparently used mushrooms and other plants to induce intoxication and hallucination, as well as for medicinal purposes. Archeological evidence dates beer production as early as 6000 B.C. However, there have always been social controls on psychoactive drugs to prevent their abuse.

In America controlling drug abuse has been a continuous problem. Taxing alcohol led to the Whiskey Rebellion in 1794, and temperance unions formed as early as 1826 to fight alcohol abuse. In the nineteenth century cocaine and morphine were commonly used in over-the-counter drugs with a resultant high addiction rate, and in 1914 the Harrison Act prohibited the sale of narcotics except by prescription. Alcohol was nationally prohibited between 1919 and 1933. In 1937 the popularity of marijuana led to its legal ban. Control of tobacco has escalated since 1964 when smoking was officially linked to lung cancer. In 1970 the Comprehensive Drug Abuse and Prevention Control Act redefined drugs according to potential for use and abuse, and in 1986 even more drug laws provided monies for drug enforcement, treatment, and education.

This long war on drugs has had mixed results. Drug abuse rises and falls in cycles not easily influenced by legislative measures as the popularity of various drugs waxes and wanes. In 1920 there were 500,000 morphine and cocaine addicts; by 1945 there were a tenth that number. In 1960 the recreational use of hallucinogens skyrocketed, dropped in the 1980s, and then rose in the 1990s. Heroin addiction has been remarkably constant in numbers, unaffected by efforts of law enforcement.

In this lesson, students examine drug abuse and prevention. They make judgments about the value of education, regulation, punishment, and the advice of some experts to legalize drugs altogether.

Understanding the Reading

Following a reading of the book review that follows, students should be able to answer the following questions:

1. How does Mr. Addison define *drug abuse*? (the use of any drug to the point that it causes negative effects in a person's physical, mental, or social life)

2. Why did people in the nineteenth century become addicted to narcotic drugs? (because cocaine and morphine were commonly used in nonprescription drugs and morphine was the only available painkiller)

3. How does Mr. Addison believe America should combat its drug problem? (by legalizing drugs)

4. What are the three arguments Mr. Addison states in favor of legalizing drugs? (doing so will not increase drug use, imprisoning drug offenders is ineffective, alcohol and tobacco are more dangerous than many illegal drugs)

Teaching Activities

1. Is drug testing unconstitutional? Should drugs be legalized? What is the best method of stopping the abuse of drugs in America? Ask students to decide. Divide the class into groups of three or four and assign the "Dealing with Drugs" activity.

2. Even the use of drugs for medicinal purposes can be tricky. Medicines are prescribed with specific rules for their use as well as warnings about their side effects and misuse. Require students to research the uses, side effects, and results of misuse of commonly prescribed drugs with the "Take Only as Prescribed" activity. A medical dictionary is a good place to begin the research.

Extensions

1. One hundred dollars worth of coca leaves can yield $300,000 when refined into cocaine and sold on the street. Opium selling for about $100 a kilogram has a street value of $800,000 when refined into heroin. Require students to devise a plan for encouraging countries who rely on drug trafficking for their economic health to halt the sale of drugs. What will sustain their economies?

2. Write a letter to the president of the United States outlining your class' ideas on halting the trafficking of drugs.

3. Collect and post newspaper accounts on the perils of drug abuse.

Legalization: Solving America's Drug Problem
Anthony Addison, Endzone Press

Addison, a professor at Berkeley, divides his timely book into four parts. The first three are informative and often intriguing. The fourth breezes along in the same easy style, but without sound facts and statistics.

Definitions are an important starting point in any discussion of the drug problem, and Addison begins with an excellent background in terms. He defines *drug abuse* in terms of negative effects on the physical, mental, or social life, and distinguishes it from *dependency* which involves difficulty in stopping the use of a drug. He makes no distinctions between legal and illegal drugs and contends that one can abuse alcohol as easily as cocaine.

In his book Addison highlights acts of Congress passed over the years including the Harrison Act of 1914 that prohibited the sale of narcotic drugs except by prescription, the 1970 Comprehensive Drug Abuse and Prevention Control Act, and the 1986 laws funding drug enforcement, treatment, and education.

The third section of the book covers the fascinating history of drug use and abuse in America. Here the author weaves together the Native American use of peyote in religious rituals, the morphine addiction of most surgery patients before less-addictive painkillers were found, the once-common presence of opium and cocaine in over-the-counter elixirs, the "mind expansion" counterculture of the 1960s, and the epidemics of today.

In his final section, however, Addison goes beyond fact as he asserts what he believes to be a rational solution to drug abuse. "Legalizing drugs," he says, "would eliminate much of the crime in America; addicts could be offered treatment instead of incarceration; addiction would decline to manageable numbers." But this method has not worked with alcohol and cigarettes, and in the end Addison's book fails to make its case.

Dealing with Drugs

With the members of your group, research and discuss the following questions. Have a recorder record responses so you can share your group's ideas with the entire class.

1. Assign one member of your group the reading of the Constitution and the amendments to the rest of the group. Is it constitutional to require a person to pass a drug test before being hired for a job? Use the Constitution to support your position. Should one be required to pass a drug test in order to be hired for a job or accepted into a college? Should one be submitted to random testing once employed or accepted into school? Why or why not?

2. Three reasons some experts and politicians suggest drugs should be legalized: currently illegal drugs are often less harmful than legal drugs (tobacco and alcohol), legalization will not create more users or abusers, imprisoning drug offenders does not work and wastes taxpayers' money. What do you think (as a group)? Address each of the three claims.

3. America buys 60 percent of the world's illegal drugs. What are the best methods for stopping the abuse of drugs in America? Educating people who have seldom or never used drugs? Detoxifying and educating current addicts? Arresting all drug dealers? Arresting kingpins? Placing sanctions on countries that sell drugs? Breaking up organized crime groups? Other ideas?

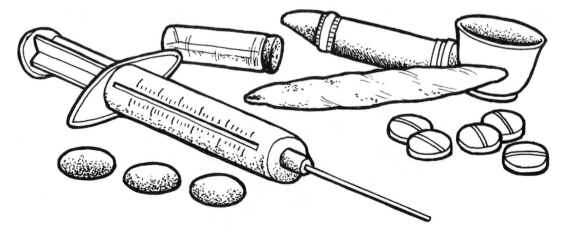

Take Only as Prescribed

Listed below are 15 commonly prescribed drugs. Although they are prescribed by a doctor, they can be quite harmful if misused and can cause side effects even when used correctly. Fill out the chart below listing each drug's use, possible side effects, and possible results if misused.

Name of Drug	Purpose of Drug	Possible Side Effects	Possible Results If Misused
Aspirin			
Sleeping pills			
Diet pills			
Laxatives			
Acetaminophen			
Ibuprofen			
Hydrocortisone			
Antidepressants			
Steroids			
Antihistamines			
Bronchodilators			
Decongestants			
Tranquilizers			
Diuretics			
Antibiotics			

Women at Work

Background

In primitive tribes the roles of women and men in providing food and shelter were probably very similar, but as settled agricultural communities evolved, the roles differentiated. Women became responsible for cooking and child-rearing while men specialized in hunting and the crude stone technologies. This separation of roles grew ever greater as civilization developed in all cultures. By 3000 B.C. women had little political or economic voice and were restricted to home and family. This pattern carried through the periods of the Roman Empire, early Christianity, the Middle Ages, the Renaissance, and the Reformation. It was not until the late eighteenth century that women began to expand their limited work and political roles in society.

With the expansion of industrialization in capitalistic democracies in the West, women began finding wage work outside of the home and marginally more legal rights and political power. Today the old-fashioned idea of distinct work roles for men and women has all but disappeared in highly developed countries. In America, 60 percent of women participate in the workplace, and those just joining the labor market earn 94 percent of what their male peers earn. Although in the 50s and 60s women held unskilled labor positions for the most part, they now hold managerial and professional positions in all kinds of fields once dominated by men. In medicine, business, and law, women make up 20 percent of the work force. Seven million women own their own businesses, and new businesses are more likely to be headed by a woman than a man.

In terms of education, all barriers have fallen. Though men still tend to dominate enrollments in a few fields like engineering and physics, there are actually more women than men in college today. Thus, women's presence in the professional workplace is almost certain to rise further in coming decades.

The "glass ceiling" effect which seems to keep women out of the male-dominated corporate board rooms seems the last obstacle for women who would like to enjoy these high-salary, powerful positions still held almost exclusively by males. Yet dramatic in-roads have been made by women in corporate management and even the glass ceiling is just a stone's throw away from falling.

In this lesson, students examine the position of women in the work force today and consider the possible future of women at work.

Understanding the Reading

Following a reading of the magazine article, students should be able to answer the following questions:

1. Although the author of this article takes a whimsical look at just who is responsible for loading and unloading the dishwasher in the homes of working women, what is the real issue she addresses? (The author addresses the issue of dividing household chores in families where the adults work.)

2. What is the glass ceiling referred to in the first paragraph of the article? (Although women today hold many managerial positions in corporate America, the executive, board room positions are still held almost exclusively by men.)

3. What would you say was the tone of this article? (This article was light and satirical. Although the author addressed a real issue, it is clear by the first paragraph, especially, that she is aware that there are much greater issues facing working women today.)

Teaching Activities

1. Although women are making their way into more and more fields that were once dominated by men, there are still some areas (especially in the maths and sciences) in which women do not often hold jobs. Challenge students to create an ad for a company that is looking for more female applicants in the "Calling All Women" activity.

2. The history of the American woman is something that could be studied for an entire semester. Allow students to get a taste of some of the important events and women behind the advancement of women in our country by choosing a specific woman or event to research or report on with the "A History of the American Woman" activity sheet. Cut out the topics along the dotted lines and require each student or group of students to research and report on one topic. Following the reports, the class may wish to create a time line of the events and people studied.

Extensions

1. Encourage students to spend a day at work with a working woman.

2. Require students to interview an at-home mom about her daily chores and activities. How does staying at home benefit a family? How does it benefit society as a whole?

3. Require students to research the role of women in other societies—especially those less-developed countries where women make up only five to ten percent of the work force. How do religion, politics, and the specific customs of various cultures affect a woman's status in a given country?

Who Loads and Unloads the Dishwasher?

There are those who will tell you that the largest obstacle for the working woman is the "glass ceiling" that separates her from the power and money of the corporate board room. Others will argue that the real challenge for the woman in the work force is exemplified in the single woman who heads a family of four, holds a low-paying unskilled labor position, and struggles to pay the rent and put food on the table. I do not deny that these working women issues deserve the news and the talk and the stories that address them. But there remains an issue that I have yet to see addressed, and to which I urgently need an answer. My question is simple—in the house of the working woman, who loads and unloads the dishwasher?

My name is Lauryl Julia and I am the chief executive secretary in charge of professional development at the Ryen Mackay Data Base Corporation. I have a good job and a great home life. When I arrive home at the end of a satisfying day of work, I cook dinner. My two teenage kids clean the house. My husband washes the clothes. Occasionally, we have to negotiate whether the family car is going to spend the day in the parking lot of an office supply store, a baseball diamond, or the mall, but we usually find some way for the faithful vehicle to get everyone where everyone wants to be. The one we really fight about is—who is going to take care of the dishwasher?

It was easy in the 1950s when my parents were raising me. No one needed a job list to see whose day it was to take out the garbage. No one needed a calendar to see where the family car would spend the day. Mom stayed home and did home stuff. Dad went to work and did work stuff. The baseball diamond and the movie theater were both within walking distance.

Today it is more of a challenge. When all of the adults in a home (whether that be one, two, or many) work outside of the home, it is difficult to decide just how all of the household things will get done. If you have found the answer in your house, let me know. The dishes are really beginning to pile up.

Calling All Women

Although women can be found in nearly any job these days, there are some professions and businesses that have far fewer women than men. Imagine you are an advertising consultant for a company or profession that would like to create an advertisement for the *Women Who Work Magazine* which encourages women to apply for a position in your company or profession. Write the slogan and other words you will use and draw a picture that will encourage women to apply for the job.

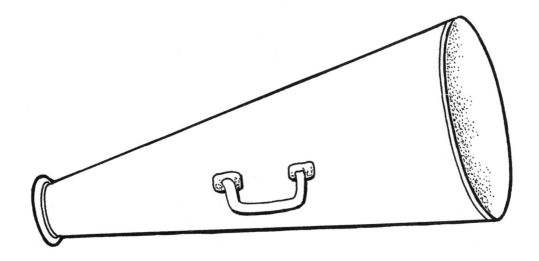

A History of the American Woman

Teacher: Separate the following topics by cutting along the dotted lines. Place the topics in a cup. Allow students to choose a topic to research and report on before the class. Following a presentation of all the reports, have students create a time line of events and important people in the history of women in America.

- -

CARRIE CHAPMAN

- -

ALICE PAUL

- -

ELEANOR ROOSEVELT

- -

CIVIL RIGHTS ACT

- -

EQUAL RIGHTS AMENDMENT

- -

SENECA FALLS CONVENTION

- -

FOURTEENTH AMENDMENT

- -

SANDRA DAY O'CONNOR

- -

SUSAN B. ANTHONY

- -

ELIZABETH CADY STANTON

- -

LUCY STONE

- -

SALLY RIDE

- -

NINETEENTH AMENDMENT

- -